Just a Few Feet from Hell

JANEL HESSON

ISBN 978-1-0980-5851-7 (hardcover)
ISBN 978-1-0980-5852-4 (digital)

Cover Design in part by Joann Shipperbottom

Christian Faith Publishing, Inc.
832 Park Avenue
Meadville, PA 16335
www.christianfaithpublishing.com

Printed in the United States of America

That House

It was a long time ago, a lifetime really, and yet with a single careless thought, I am suddenly back in that house—in that moment, on that night.

Yes, that night is seared into my memory, permanently etched on to my brain, as if it was yesterday. Every detail—the dimly lit lighting casting a yellow glow over the front entrance of the house, where the people were standing, the TV on in the other room. You see, things had been going bad for me in that house for quite some time. It was where my parents brought me for babysitting when they went out on Friday nights and during the day when they went to work, thinking they had brought me somewhere safe, for we were related to these people—which is probably why they didn't believe me when I started to protest. My babysitter, who was a great deal older than me, was molesting me, and during the day, his younger sister (she was a year older than me) terrorized me.

So what made that night different? A couple of things—for one, I had made up my mind. I was six years old, and I would not spend one more night in that house with him, who had already warned me not to speak a word, or he would hurt me. I was standing in the entryway, he was directly behind me, his sister was a little behind and off my left shoulder, my dad was directly in front of me, and my mom was to my right. I was begging them to please not leave me here, tears streaming down my face.

My mom asked me, "Why shouldn't we leave you?"

Fear gripped me as my babysitter loomed over me from behind, waiting for my response. I was unable to speak, and my crying turned to uncontrollable sobbing, and in between sobs, I pleaded, "Please don't leave me!" I looked up at my mom, who seemed a little concerned, and then to my dad, who stared down at me with complete contempt and disgust in his eyes. His anger toward me was so intense I thought his eyes might burn a hole right through me. Now not only was I scared but confused. Why was he so angry? What had I done? But before I could think another thought, something happened that sent shivers down my spine and haunts me to this day.

As my dad stood glaring down at me with a very tangible anger, quite suddenly his very blue eyes turned black! I mean completely black—no pupils, no white, just black! A blackness so intense, so real, it went right through me, straight to my soul. I had—and never have seen since—hatred like that. A hatred so unspeakable, so penetrating, it seemed to suck the life and breath right out of my body, leaving me paralyzed to do anything. A profound sense of terror and dread came upon me, and I was unable to look away from those eyes and that blackness. Then just as quickly as it had appeared, it was gone, and then so was my dad. He threw open the front door and stormed out of that house.

As the door slammed shut behind him, I looked to my mom, hoping she would scoop me up in her arms, tell me everything would be okay, take me with her, and never bring me to that house again, but without a word or even a hug, she left too. And there I stood alone in that house with him again.

I had been so sure that this time would be different, that this time they would listen to my crying and begging and would know that something was wrong. They would realize how unusual this behavior was. Surely, they would see how their normally happy, laughing little girl was obviously distraught about something. Didn't they wonder why I never cried when we were at home on our farm? How happy I was riding my pony and playing with my dog? How I didn't cause trouble and how crying was reserved only for being injured? But they didn't; they just left. It was devastating. That night would be the last time I would ever cry and ask them for help—ever.

That night would also mark the beginning of many years of abuse and torture for me. Knowing now that I was too scared to say anything and that my parents didn't believe me, my babysitter felt free to abuse at will, and his sister began her own form of abuse—

doing things like grabbing one of my arms with both her hands and squeezing as hard as she could, digging her fingernails into my skin until I was bleeding.

The first time it happened, I cried out in pain. Her mother heard me and came into the room. Thinking she had come to help me, I was glad to see her, but it was just the opposite. Seeing what was happening, she grabbed me by my other arm, jerked me away violently, and began to spank me severely, yelling at me at the same time, "Don't you ever upset my daughter like that again!"

Uh, wait a minute, I didn't do anything to your daughter. In fact, I was just sitting there playing by myself when she came in and grabbed me. I tried to tell the mother this, but it only angered her more, and the spanking turned into a beating. This became a way of life at that house. The daughter would scratch me, knock me down, hit me, cut me, drawing blood most times, but it still didn't matter, and if I did or said anything, the mother would come and beat me. In the times I was bleeding and needed a Band-Aid, I would have to go to the mother and tell her I hurt myself and "could I please have a Band-Aid?" She would yell about my carelessness and jerk me around a little, but that was much better than the beatings.

I learned to endure the pain in silence. The only thing worse than the abuse was my own mother's complete lack of concern. She saw the cuts, scratches, and bruises, and she did nothing, said nothing—in fact, all she ever said was to try not to upset her so. What? Like I had done something to provoke this? I did nothing to that girl except tippy-toe around her like I was on eggshells, trying desperately to stay out of her way and just get along. Unfortunately, no matter what I did or how hard I tried, she always found a way to hurt me. Sensing my mistrust in her, she would be very nice, laughing and playing like normal for long periods of time—long enough for me to drop my guard—and then she would get me. Other times, she would fake being hurt by me and call out for her mother, who would appear promptly, spanking me so hard I thought I wouldn't survive. All the while, the girl would watch in pleasure with a very evil smile on her face—a smile I can still see to this day. This was how it went day in and day out. If it wasn't physical abuse, it was mental. "Do what I say, or I will call my mom. Do exactly what I want, or I will call my mom," there was no relief. And then Friday night would come, and I would be left with him.

The spankings were so severe they left me completely bruised—all purple and red. It made sitting down for a bath nearly unbearable. I would just sit there quietly, whimpering, wondering why my mom didn't care. She saw the bruises, why was nothing done? Why did she keep taking me back? Why didn't she believe me? These are horrible thoughts for a six-year-old, and even more disturbing was that she just kept saying, "You need to be more careful. Don't upset the girl, and then this won't happen." I knew, though, that this wasn't my fault. I never did anything to those people that justified them treating me this way. I never doubted myself for a second, but I did start doubting my parents. It was very clear that no matter what happened or what I said, they were never going to believe me. They would always side with everyone else. My confidence faded away as I realized that the two people in the whole world who are supposed to protect me at all costs weren't going to. Through their actions, or lack thereof, they made it abundantly clear that my opinion didn't matter, what I wanted didn't matter—I didn't matter! I felt alone and insignificant. However, at six years old, I was not able to verbalize or even really process these thoughts and feelings, so I withdrew into me and into a darkness that would follow me everywhere always.

Years went by with no relief until finally my babysitter moved away to go to college, and I finally convinced my mother that, at ten years old, I did not need babysitting anymore! It worked, and for the first time in years, summer days were great again! Different but great—different because I found myself longing to be alone with my animals and as far from people as possible. We lived in a very rural area, which made this easy to do. I spent all day outside playing with my dog or just hanging out with the horses. I mean that literally. I spent so much time with them that I had become one of the herd.

We had around five horses at that time, one of which was two years old. She was still too young to be trained to ride, so no one had ever sat on her back. But I had spent so much time just sitting with them as they grazed and walking around among them that I was simply accepted as one of them. So one day, as they had entered the corral where the waterer was, I was sitting on the feed trough as they milled around, each waiting for their turn to take a drink. The two-year-old that had never been ridden was standing beside me, and with the advantage of being up on the feeder, I simply slid onto her back. There was no fear, no concern on her part. In fact, all she did was turn and sniff my toes. I was always barefoot on the farm and could run on rocks as well as the grass. For those of you who don't know horses, usually the first time they have a person on their back can cause absolute terror and panic, usually resulting in a frenzied attempt to buck the person off. But so accepted was I that she had no fear of me, no concern whatsoever. It became a daily thing—I would get her to stand by the feeder and then climb onto her back and sit there while they grazed for hours at a time. And when I got tired of sitting, I simply leaned back and lay on her back, hands folded under my head like a pillow, and watched the clouds float by.

One day, while watching the clouds go by, I must have fallen asleep, for all of a sudden, I felt some jostling going on. Opening my eyes to see what was happening, I realized they had walked all the way from the pasture where they had been grazing to the corral to get a drink of water. The movement I felt was her getting a place in line for a drink. Sound asleep on a two-year-old's back—no saddle, no bridle, not even a halter. Finally, I had found where I belonged.

Mom would eventually have to come looking for me and make me come in for supper. Yup, those were great days, except horror was never far away. Being related to these people meant holidays and cookouts together. All those years of being abused by him and then having to sit next to him, her, and the mother for Christmas Eve supper, Easter dinner, Fourth of July barbecue—on and on it went. Sitting next to the very people who inflicted so much pain on me—physical and mental—and my parents completely unaware and uncaring. That's a lot of pressure for a six-, seven-, eight-, nine-year-old. So much so that by age ten, I had a full-blown ulcer, which went undiagnosed until I was sixteen.

I remember vividly one such get-together. It was summer, and we were grilling hamburgers at that house. It was too hot to sit outside, so while the men were out grilling, we women were inside getting things ready, setting the table, etc. The mother asked me to go out and ask the men what they wanted to drink, so I opened the sliding glass door and, holding onto the frame of the door with my right hand, stepped out and started asking what each of them wanted. While I was doing this, the sister, now fourteen, and I, then thirteen, came along and, very much on purpose, slammed the door shut on my fingers and locked it!

I screamed out in pain and tried to open it, but it was locked. I turned and looked at my dad, thinking he might do something. Instead, he just sat there, legs crossed and looking straight into my eyes, took a drink of his beer. I turned back to the door and started pounding on it with my left hand, desperate to get my finger free. My mom heard and came over and finally realized what was wrong. She got it open to find my middle finger smashed—the tip of it nearly cut off. It was already dark purple and bleeding bad, and it was clear I would lose that fingernail. My mom, although she seemed mad and asked the sister why she would do such a thing, never did anything more than run some cold water on my finger and then put a Band-Aid on it. Of course, the mother just played it off as an accident, and my dad, well, he never did anything. He never said a word, never asked me if I was okay, and certainly never defended me. This was my world and how my life went—me sitting next to my tormentors in silence, finger throbbing, and nobody doing anything about it.

That family tortured and abused me every time I was around them, and now it happened right in front of my parents, and they still did nothing. They did nothing to stand up for me, help me, or protect me in any way. While they might not be doing anything, I was. I was growing a resentment toward them that was intense and would continue for many, many years. Once again, their actions confirmed that I didn't really matter, and although at the time I didn't realize it, the psychological effects of this would prove to be devastating.

I slipped further and further into despair, as all hope faded that things would ever be any different. Darkness seemed to be all around, and as I sat there at that table in a great deal of pain from my finger, a new thought invaded my mind. Maybe they were right, and everything was my fault. I tried to fight it off. I mean, I didn't do anything to these people, but still there it was right in front of me. They saw what she did, and yet nothing was done about it. Why else wouldn't they help me? This thought that had just crept in made my head reel, and I became nauseous. I felt like I was falling—falling down into a deep dark pit. This one new thought brought in a multitude of more dark thoughts, like, why bother anymore? No one cares about you. You don't matter. I tried hard to ignore them, but I was getting tired, and it seemed each thought just pushed me further down into this pit I had fallen into and further into darkness. It seemed as though the darkness was winning as it slowly choked out all light, all happiness, all hope.

I'm not sure I can describe to you just how dark my world had become. I didn't really laugh anymore, talk very much, or even hear the birds sing. My thoughts had turned heavy and oppressive, smothering the life right out of me. There was no joy or peace anymore. All the things I used to enjoy just weren't fun anymore. Laughing became a forced response at the proper time. I was going through the motions of living on the outside while dying on the inside.

At first, there had been so many questions. Why? Why didn't they help me? Why didn't they listen to me? Slowly the darkest thought of all had wormed its way into my thinking. It must be me. I must be bad. I must be doing something wrong. Why else wouldn't they help me? A mental battle had begun. I didn't do anything to these people. For God's sake, I was only six years old! Yet still there it was—the complete dislike in Dad's eyes, my mom saying nothing about the marks on my arms. I mean, could it be...was it really all my fault?

By age fifteen, my mind was destroying itself, trying to rationalize what had been happening to me and why my parents didn't seem to really care about me. I was just a little kid, what could I have possibly done that was so bad to make them treat me this way? The thoughts were so overwhelming that I just couldn't deal with them anymore. Unknowingly, my mind dropped into survival mode. If you don't talk about something, then it's like it never really happened. So that's exactly what I did—pretend it didn't happen, and it didn't. The older I got, the better I got at this, and I would become the master of denial. It worked, too, for a while.

Although denying things was working on the outside, no one had any idea anything was wrong. It was destroying me on the inside. The voice in my head could not be shut out by denial. It was a constant, unceasing reminder that I was bad, it's all my fault, no one really cares, and, worst of all, I'm insignificant. It just never shut up, always accusing me, always reminding me that things would never get better, never change. There's no way out, and you will never be anything.

Hold up, wait a minute, voice. I don't care what you say. I have dreams I will be a horse trainer with my own beautiful farm. I didn't know it at the time, but that one thought, that one dream of being a professional horse trainer would be the one thing that would keep me from complete self-destruction.

I was becoming more and more desperate, however, to silence that voice in my head. The only relief I got was when I was asleep, but as soon as my eyes opened in the morning, before I could even get my feet on the floor, there it was with a barrage of dark gloomy, hopeless thoughts.

Being fifteen brought with it new challenges of its own—how to fit in now that I was in junior high, making new friends, and just trying to get along with others in this world. That's when I met a boy. He was nice and paid a lot of attention to me—in a good way! He was very gentle and kind, carrying my books between classes and opening doors for me. Wow, someone who was nice to me, who actually seemed to like me! It was refreshing, invigorating—unbelievable how my luck had changed! Or so it seemed.

We spent hours talking on the phone, just being teenagers. Talking to him was a great way to drown out the voice, and having someone who seemed to like me kind of made me feel better about me, at least while we were talking. It was a wonderful time for me, right up until everything changed.

Now sixteen, he had his driver's license, and on a Friday night, he came to take me to a movie. However, he had other intentions in mind. As we drove toward the town where the theater was, he turned abruptly down a side road that led back to some trees. It was a dark and deserted place, just out in a field with trees and with no one around for miles. Putting the car in park, he climbed over onto me and my seat and began kissing and touching me. Instantaneously, I was back in that house—six years old and paralyzed by fear. Something rose up in me, though, as new thoughts came pouring in. *He's not my babysitter. I'm not six anymore. This is not going to happen!*

As soon as I started to protest, the once kind and gentle boy I knew turned into an angry, violent stranger. He was bigger, stronger, and already on top of me. I was unable to stop him. When he was finished, he looked at me and said, "You're mine now, and I'm going to marry you."

Keep quiet, I thought to myself. *Just agree with him so he will take you home.* So I nodded in agreement.

He did eventually take me home. When I got out of the car, I turned and looked in at him, saying, "Don't come near me ever again. We are through." Then I slammed the door shut and ran into my house. As usual, my dad was asleep, and my mom was watching TV. I had to go past her to get to my bedroom.

"How was the movie?" she asked.

"Fine," I replied.

"Did you have fun?"

"Yes." I was past her now, down the hall and into my room. I wasn't going to tell her anything. She wouldn't believe me, anyway. She never has, why would she now? She would just get mad and tell me what I already knew—it's all my fault; it always is. I should never have gone with him, I should never have trusted him.

Things appeared fine for the remainder of the weekend; there were no phone calls or visits from him. I thought I had successfully stood up for myself and that it had actually worked! Or did it?

Monday came, and my life would never be the same again. Back in school and having to see my once "knight in shining armor," things went from bad to worse. He told everyone, told them everything—well, not quite everything. He forgot to mention how he violently forced himself on me. No, he had a very different version of how things went, and everyone was quick to believe him. No one even asked me if it was true. Not even one of my so-called friends came to my defense. Nope, they just all jumped on board and started whispering behind my back, staring at me, pointing fingers, and calling me names. It seemed useless to try and defend myself or tell my version of the story. I mean, my parents never believed me, so why would these people? It was horrible—the condemning looks of disapproval, people I thought were my friends turning on me. School had been like a place of refuge for me, a place where I felt safe and accepted, for I had made friends quickly and easily. Now it had become just like that house—a place of darkness and torment.

By Friday, things came to a head, and the guy who used to be nice to me had me cornered in a in a hall, yelling at me. I should say screaming. His face was red and distorted, his eyes flashing as he told me how he had expected to marry me, that I was the one for him and how much he loved me! Then he blurted out, "If I can't have you, I'm going to kill myself," and with that, he ran out of the building.

My head started reeling, and I felt that feeling of falling again, deeper into the pit of despair. I left school feeling numb, not sure what to do or what to believe. Was he really going to kill himself? Should I tell someone? Do I care?

The weight of my dark world was crushing down on me, and I wasn't sure how long I could stand up under it. Later that night, I got a call from one of the few people who would still talk to me. She said there was a party going on at a classmate's house and asked if I wanted to go. No, I was not in the party mood, but she convinced me it would be good for me to get out of the house and get my mind off things.

We got there and headed down to the basement where everyone was at, and there he was, very much alive, laughing and drinking, having a great time. It was right then at that moment things became very clear to me. People lie, people hurt you, they will not help you, and they absolutely cannot be trusted.

I asked my friend if we could leave. She agreed, and as I climbed back up the stairs, it felt as though my shoes were made of cement. Again the weight of things made it nearly impossible to get back up a simple flight of stairs, and when I finally did, I stepped into the living room. As if things couldn't get any worse, there she was—the sister who had terrorized me most of my young life. She was on the couch having sex with some guy. She just looked up at me as I walked by and smiled the same twisted, evil smile that I knew all too well.

I left that place feeling worse than before and, not caring what we did next, agreed to drive to a nearby town to see if anyone was around. We found some guys who were hanging out, drinking beer. You have to remember we were in a very rural area. Towns were tiny, and with one local cop, it was easy to avoid detection. We joined them. One of the guys offered me a beer. I hesitated. I was fifteen and driving on a learner's permit, but my friend, who was already drinking, told me, "Drink it and I promise you'll feel better." So I did, and she was right! It was awesome!

Saturday morning wasn't very fun. I have never had a headache like that before, but as far as I was concerned, it was worth it to feel that good for even a couple hours!

Beauty

During this time of growing up and with all these things happening to me, my parents had done one thing right: they bought me a pony. I was five, and her name was Beauty. I will never forget about that night. It was almost Christmas, and my parents picked me up from school, a one-room country school. With only seven of us in the entire school and me the only one in my grade, it was great! Of course, I didn't know anything different. It was just country life, and I loved it!

I had actually wanted a friend to stay over with me on this Friday night, and I was quite upset when their answer was no. They said they had somewhere to go, and since my older brother was with us, it was crowded as I climbed into our white Chevy truck with racks on the back and onto my mom's lap.

It was a foggy December day as we started driving on what seemed like an impossibly long trip to me. The sun had long since gone down when we finally reached our destination. As we pulled into the lane, we drove into a farm with a large white farmhouse and an even larger white barn. There was a tall post in the area between the house and the barn with an outdoor light on it, big enough to light up the whole area.

As we were getting out of the truck, a man emerged from the house pulling on a heavy winter coat, smiling as he came and greeted my dad with a handshake. Still smiling, he looked down at me and asked, "Do you want to see something?"

I remember looking straight up at this man, who seemed like a giant to me, and nodding yes.

He said, "Then come with me."

We walked toward the barn, and with one big motion, he slid open the large white door, upon which I heard a commotion break out in the darkness of the barn. When he turned on the light, I was able to see what was making all that commotion—two huge white mules, and then there she was, the most beautiful brown pony I had ever seen.

When the three of them settled down, the pony stood between the two large mules, all three looking intently at us. The big man looked down at me again and asked, "Do you want to ride her?" Barely believing what I was seeing and was now hearing, I whispered yes. He got a bridle on the pony and led her out of the barn and into the area between the house and the barn, and before I could do or say anything, he reached down with one arm and swept me up and onto her back. Immediately, I could feel the warmth of her body under me, and when I asked her to go, I could feel every muscle and all the power she had in her little body. That was it, I was in love.

I rode her all around the light post near our truck. Everywhere the light reached, I rode her. The big man was laughing now as he looked at my dad, saying, "I think she's hooked!" And with that, my dad bought the pony named Beauty. She came with a bridle, a cart, and a harness. No saddle, but that was fine; I didn't need one. Beauty was trained to jump, so the man led her to the back of our pickup. Dad dropped the tailgate, and without hesitating, she jumped right in, and away we went! Best day ever!

When we got her home and settled in our barn, I needed a lot of convincing to leave her! Just sure she would disappear overnight, I had made up my mind to sleep with her. Unbothered with the cold, I was too excited to even notice it was cold out! I begrudgingly gave in and went to bed in the house, but with the light of day, I was up dressed and running toward the barn. I struggled with the large door, but with great determination, I slid it open, rushed in, and there she was—alive and as real as the night before. It wasn't a dream after all!

Beauty would become my best friend, my only real friend, my whole world. She would save me in ways I'm still realizing today! Every moment of every day I wasn't in school or in that house, I spent with her! And once I was finally free from my babysitter, we

15

were inseparable! I would get on that pony in the morning and leave—leave all day, leave everyone and everything behind—only returning as the sun was going down. Not only did Beauty give me the gift of love, but riding her also gave me a new sense of freedom. If and when I did want to play with my friends (the other kids who went to the one-room country school), I simply got on Beauty and rode to their house, some of which were close to ten miles away! I just got up early, rode to their place, played all day, just making sure to leave with enough time to get home before the sun went down. That was my mom's only rule: be home before dark. It was like being able to drive a car at six years old, and this new freedom made feel powerful, in control, when the rest of my world was so out of control. She was my salvation—my one bright spot in an otherwise very dark world. With her, there was simply no condemnation, no judging, only love, absolute and unconditional love. Everything I needed was found in her—safety, acceptance, strength, and, the one thing I was most desperate for, love. Yes, living on a farm in such a rural area was definitely a gift from God, so much so that I'm still realizing it all these years later.

I was able to ride down the road and almost never see a car or a person, just an occasional farmer out checking fences or livestock. Driveways were long and farmers were busy working on their farms, and most of the women stayed home, raising their kids and helping on the farm. Country life was heaven on earth for me! It was also the reason my dad bought two young horses. They would be my brother's project; he would teach them to ride when they got old enough. He had bought the horses for him and my brother to ride, but unknowingly, he had just bought my second best friend.

As I grew older and bigger, it was becoming obvious that I wouldn't be able to keep riding Beauty. I did not want to let go of the bond that had developed between us, for in her presence was such love and trust and something I couldn't quite put my finger on. Maybe it was that when I was around her, I felt safe, protected, maybe even a little bit happy? The only thing I did know for sure was that there was something about her that made me feel good about me.

All too soon, I realized me riding her had become a burden to her. Even though Beauty never objected, never walked away from me, my size just made it very hard on her. I knew I could ride her no longer.

In the meantime, one of those young horses was now three, and my brother was riding her some. He decided it was time for me to start riding her. Reluctantly, I did. Her name was Agi Pat. Born of world champion bloodlines, she would soon become my champion. She would take over where Beauty left off, and once again, I was riding for hours at a time all over the countryside, leaving in the morning and only to return in the evening. During one of those rides, I discovered something about Agi Pat. She was fast—freakish fast! So if we weren't flying down the side of the road, wind whipping in our hair, we were quietly walking, just enjoying the sights and sounds of country living. Those rides were the best moments of my life. They were the only reason I got up in the mornings, the only reason I kept breathing for one more day. They had become all that I lived for. If you've never ridden a horse or had a connection with one, it might be hard for you to understand, but there is something unexplainable about them, and once you've experienced it, it's intoxicating.

Growing up, horses represented everything I felt I wasn't but wanted to be. They are powerful, courageous, and noble. At six years old, I was powerless to help myself. I was scared all the time, and I saw myself as insignificant and unworthy. But put me on a horse, and instantly their strength made me feel strong, their courage made me brave, and their unconditional love made me feel valuable, needed, loved. I relished in their great strength, and I basked in their love! I spent every moment I could with these horses, gaining their trust and respect and earning a place in their herd. I loved them, and they loved me. I would do anything for them, and they would do anything for me. Being around them was the only time I felt like I belonged, like I was accepted and there was no judging. They simply loved me exactly the way I was.

I never rode with a saddle, only bareback, just like that night many years before when I rode Beauty for the first time, for it allowed me to feel her great strength even more. So I would ride all day every day. Hot or cold, it didn't matter; those long quiet rides were like a drug I had to have. They were the only time when I didn't have to pretend—pretend I was all right, pretend I was happy. No, Agi Pat loved and accepted me just the way I was, broken and all.

Those rides would sustain me in the midst of the darkness that had become my reality. As time went on, our relationship would develop into a love I can't explain. My love for her was so strong, my commitment to her so undeniable, that it would one day save my life. Literally.

Tragedy

I must take a moment here and tell you that there were some good times with my parents. My mom would take me on shopping trips to a town about twenty miles from us. It was the only town big enough to have a small shopping mall and a McDonald's. I loved those trips. Having Mom all to myself, it made me feel special. We had also started showing our horses, so my parents, brother, and I would travel to these shows and have a good time. Things always seemed better when we were away from that family, but for me, no matter how far we traveled, the darkness followed me—a heaviness that I could never shake. I had determined, though, if you don't speak about something out loud, it meant it never really happened. So I said nothing and became really good at appearing normal.

Tragedy struck when I was eleven. My parents sold the farm—our farm, my farm. My sanctuary and refuge. And wouldn't you know it, they moved me into town and exactly one block from that house! To say I was devastated would be a gross understatement, and no matter how much I pleaded and begged them not to, they did it, anyway. No surprise, same story. Not even sure why I tried, but I was desperate not to lose the only place I felt safe, the only place I felt out of reach by that family. Even if they showed up, I just got on my horse and left.

At least, they brought the horses with us. We had several now. They built their house on the edge of town with three acres outside of city limits for the barn and all of the animals I had accumulated. I had every kind of pet imaginable—cats, dogs owls, pigeons, a goose, baby calf, opossums (yes, opossums), rabbits, you name it. If I could get my hands on them, they came home with me! By the time we moved to town, I was down to just cats, dogs, rabbits, and the horses.

I love animals—all animals—and more importantly, they loved me back! They're always there for you, always glad to see you, and they never, ever turn on you.

The whole reason we had moved to this rural area was so that my dad could work for/with the father of that family, the leader of all that evil, and as time went on, he made life for my dad miserable. The father was president of the business, and my dad was made vice president, and it became clear to my dad he had gone into business with a crooked man. He lied, made bad deals, cheated people, and would eventually start stealing money from the business and clients. He even began laundering money through Vegas. There was simply no end to his corruption.

My dad unfortunately did not know about all that he was doing, for he had brought in a new partner, and the two of them were really good at keeping secrets. He only knew that he was making bad deals that were bringing the business down. If my dad only knew just how far down this man would eventually bring us all. My dad felt trapped. We had only moved to this town for this job. His previous job had him moving all the time, which, now that his kids were getting older, was just too hard on the family. So not wanting to move again, he had decided to stick it out. So to deal with his unhappy life, he started drinking—drinking a lot—and then he started taking things out on me.

Six months had gone by since I had broken things off with the boyfriend. Life was going on. I hated every minute of every day of school. It was a constant onslaught of accusations, name-calling, and finger-pointing. I literally counted the days, hours, and minutes left till I would graduate. In the midst of this, something new was happening to me. I started having debilitating leg cramps and never-ending nosebleeds. The cramps would wake me up in the middle of the night, causing me to scream in such pain that sometimes I would wake my mom. The nosebleeds came every day, several times a day, each time lasting longer and coming more frequently—until finally, one day, as I was leaving school, I had another one that just wouldn't stop. It bled all the way home on the bus and the walk from the bus stop to my house. It wasn't letting up. In fact, by the time I got into my home, blood was pouring out of my nose like a water faucet. Forget about a tissue, I grabbed a hand towel. I tried tipping my head back, but it poured down my throat, choking me and making me gag. It was like drinking blood. Nothing I was doing was helping or slowing the flow of blood, so I eventually just stood there, leaning my head over my sink, watching the blood flow for so long. I got tired, so I got a washcloth, folded it up, and laid it on the edge of the bathtub. I sat down, put my cheek on it, positioning my nose so the blood would run into the tub, and then just let it run. That's where my mom found me when she got home from work, unconscious and still bleeding.

She started shaking me and yelling at me to wake up. I vaguely remember trying to pick my head up, trying to stand up, but I was too weak and just wanted to close my eyes and sleep. My mom called my dad and made him come home immediately to help. He carried me to my bed, and Mom placed several bath towels under my head and nose. Not realizing the severity of the situation, they waited till morning to take me to the doctor. The doctor took one look at me and rushed right in to doing tests. I was pale weak and shaky on my feet. The results were back; I was pregnant. You could have heard a pin drop in that room as the weight of the doctor's words hit me and my parents like a freight train.

The doctor broke the silence. "There's something else you need to understand. The reason she (me) has been having those leg cramps and nosebleeds is because her body is too physically immature to be pregnant. In other words, being pregnant is killing her."

That's where things started to go black for me. I had that feeling of falling again, and my head started spinning as I tried to grasp what he just said. The doctor continued, "If she tries to carry the baby full term, she will for sure die. We might be able to save the child. If we perform an abortion right now, I give her a fifty-fifty chance of survival." Then he added, "Hopefully she won't bleed to death."

That's when my mom asked to speak to the doctor alone, so they left the room, leaving me alone with my thoughts, which came in faster than I could process. *First, I'm pregnant, and then I'm going to die too. What about my dream of training horses? It's all gone—gone because of a monster who forced himself on me.* Of course, no one knew that. I hadn't told anyone. They wouldn't believe me, anyway. It was system overload, and my mind, my whole body shut down.

My mom reentered the room, and without asking me anything like "Are you all right?" "How are you feeling?" or "What do you want to do?" she just informed me that she had made arrangements for an abortion.

A few days later, I found myself at a different hospital and alone in another room. Nurses were coming in and out, getting me ready for the procedure. They were rude and short with me. I knew exactly what they were thinking, how they were judging me. They had already made up their mind about me, how I was a bad person—yes, it was easy to see right there in their eyes. Funny how people form an opinion about you without all the facts, how they label you and condemn you as judge and jury. They had no idea of what I had gone through—for years—no idea of what really happened, and they didn't care. If they had, maybe they would have looked a little closer, maybe even asked, "What happened?" Nope, they just glared at me with looks of disapproval. What they really didn't know, though, was that they didn't have to look at me like that—I already knew. Yup, I already knew I was a bad person. The voice in my head had been telling me that for years.

Nothing was explained to me. I wasn't told what to expect, how things would go, or even exactly what was about to happen. Without going into details, I can tell you that it was horrible, horrific, and the most agonizing night of my life. What followed in the morning when it was through was the tipping point for me. The process of being "cleaned out" to prevent any infection was when I stopped living. And every day after that, I simply existed, went through the motions, looked like I was living, but the darkness had won. The doctor scraped out more than afterbirth that day—he took with it any feelings that remained, what little joy or hope that had been left, only to leave me a dark empty void.

A few days later, I was at home trying to recover, trying to figure out what had just happened. I was sitting at the kitchen table when there was a knock at the back door. It was a familiar voice, and quite suddenly, there he was, my abuser, home from school and just wanting to say hi. As he approached the table I was sitting at, my throat tightened. My heart started beating double time, and I immediately felt sick to my stomach. It was much worse seeing him now that I was older, for it had finally dawned on me just how sick he was, how horribly wrong it was what he had done to me.

He sat down across from me and smiled that same twisted smile and asked, "How are you?" His question nearly put me over the edge. *How am I? You know exactly how I am, you sick SOB!* I wanted to scream at him, "How dare you come into my house and even speak to me, you sick bastard!" I wanted to vent ALL of my pent-up anger, hurt, resentment, and frustration on him, scream until I could scream no more, till my voice gave out. But I didn't. I just sat there, silent, thinking to myself, *Could it get any worse?*

Finally able to speak, I politely excused myself and retreated to my bedroom, convinced that I had absolutely reached rock bottom, just sure that things could not get any worse. Of course, I was wrong. Once in my room, I lay down on my bed and cried—quietly, of course, so no one would hear.

Back in school, things did get worse. Rumors were flying, fingers were pointing, but for me, it was the looks that were the worst. People's eyes tell on them, tell what they're thinking, how they're judging you, how they don't like you. Yes, I saw it all in their eyes—every condemning, judgmental, and accusing look. No one had all the facts, no one knew what had been going on for years. I wanted to tell them, wanted to clear my name, but I was too ashamed and mostly too scared to, so I remained silent. Not one person—not my mom, not my dad, and not one of my "friends"—ever asked me about anything. Not "Is it true? Are you okay? What's your side of the story? Do you need help?" But they were all very quick to judge me, and I hated them for that.

I sank deeper into despair, retreated further into me and the darkness that had become my world, sliding ever further into the pit that I had now grown accustomed to. Every time I thought I had made it out, every time I cleared the edge—*bam*—something would blindside me, and right back over the edge I fell. Each time, it seemed the bottom was deeper. Each time, I landed a little harder. And each time, I lay there at the bottom a little longer, wondering, *Do I get up and start climbing again? Is it worth it? Do I have the strength? Do I care, or should I just lie here and die in the darkness?*

The hardest thing about being in that pit, of being knocked down, was that I didn't feel like it was my doing. I mean, I didn't try to get molested or raped. No, it seemed that everyone and everything was against me. I was just a little girl trying to grow up and now a young girl just trying to make it in this world. But still, there was that dream of mine, that insatiable love for horses, and they were worth climbing for. So I did.

As I had mentioned before, my dad had started drinking a lot and taking his frustrations out on me. He liked to be in control, and he used intimidation to gain control, which didn't work on me. I was sixteen now, and the last time I had looked up to my dad was ten years before—on that night when I was six years old. By now, I had little respect for my parents and no real use for them.

That being said, I must tell you that through all that was going on, on the outside, I appeared as normal as anyone (master of denial). I was a straight *A* student, never skipped school—even though it was a living hell for me—was in band, played the flute (second chair—second best in school) and tenor sax, played volleyball, basketball, and ran the hurdles in track. I was always polite and respectful to all of my teachers and coaches. Outside of school, I played the organ, did ballet and tap dancing, and played softball on the town's team. Doing all of the things that were expected of me. In the midst of all these activities, I was also training horses. By age eleven, I would be up at 4:00 a.m. working horses before school and then would come home and work horses after school. I did not cause trouble and I did not directly disrespect my parents. I just didn't come home on the weekends when they wanted me to.

Actually, my dad never cared when I came home. He never waited up for me or even asked where I was going. It was my mom who asked and waited up. No, it was, however, my dad who came up with his own form of abuse and what he thought would be control over me. Like I said, he was drinking a lot now, and he liked taking his pain and frustrations out on me—by killing my pets. Yes, that's what I said—killing my pets. I would go to school only to come home and find one missing. At first, I didn't understand what was happening, didn't put it together. It wasn't until I asked my dad if he knew what had happened.

The first one that went missing was a kitten I had rescued out of a gutter downtown with a horrible injury to its face. I had nursed him back to health and had gained his faithful trust and love. A sinking feeling came over me as my dad turned and looked at me. His eyes were always dark with anger whenever he looked at me, but this time, there was a new look—a very pleased, sadistic look. My eyes welled with tears as a horrific realization came upon me as his frown slowly turned into a smile. I screamed at him, "What have you done?" tears now streaming down my face as my eyes locked on his, demanding an answer.

He only smiled bigger and said, "One less mouth to feed."

I was reeling from shock and anger. My heart was breaking for the kitty I loved—who trusted me, who faithfully helped me clean stalls and do chores, who was always waiting for me when I got home from school. He was my friend, and he killed him! My own dad killed something I loved on purpose just to hurt me! I was hysterical by now, yelling and screaming, demanding an answer as to why, but the more upset I got, the more pleased he seemed, just smiling and laughing at me. It was more than my mind could handle. I couldn't process it!

Eventually, I just turned and ran to the barn and to my horses. As I entered the pen, they knew immediately something was wrong. They encircled me, each one stretching out their necks and touching my cheeks with their muzzles, gently rubbing my face as if to wipe the tears away, comforting me in the only way they knew how.

Coming home from school had once been such a great relief to me—finally away from those people for another day, soaking in all the love and excitement of my animals when they saw me! But now dread was the only thing I felt as I walked from the bus stop to my home. As each day, one by one, he took all that I loved from me.

Each cat, each rabbit, and then even my dog. The day I came home and my dog did not come running to greet me, I lost it. I met him at his truck when he got home from work, and this time, I wasn't crying. Anger and hatred spewed out of my mouth, so much so that his pleased looked turned to one of shock.

He finally broke in and told me, "I haven't killed your dog. I gave her to a guy who wanted a guard dog." My dog was a big German shepherd mix, so big that her name was Tanker. His words stunned me for a minute. I mean, I was relieved to know that she was still alive, but yet he gave her to someone else? And when he told me who, I was horrified. I knew this man, knew of how little he respected animals, the law, or the people! He was an arrogant creep that made my skin crawl every time I was around him! And as I *stood there, trying to process things*, matters got worse, for that man himself came driving into our driveway!

Thinking he had come to gloat, I barely looked his way, but then I heard his words. He had come to tell my dad that the dog— wouldn't even call her by name—had run away. He had been having trouble with her; he couldn't touch her. She growled and snarled, and when he tried tying her to a tree, she fought it so bad he thought she would either hurt herself or get away, so he locked her in his garage. And when he got home that day and went in to his garage through a side door, she was waiting. He took one step in, and she hit him so hard she knocked him to the ground and escaped. He had come to let my dad know so we could watch for her. If she came back, he would come for her. That's when he got my full attention and every- thing I thought of him and that he would NEVER get MY dog back. She was mine, and he was going to have to fight me for her.

I guess dogs were my dad's one soft spot; he had been unable to kill her and so had spared her life. The fact that she had run away gave me hope of her return, but this man lived a long way from us, out in the country. She had never been on her own to find food or water, and there were many coyotes in the area. I was distraught and terrified for her. I think even my dad was concerned. He put word out to all the farmers to be on the lookout for her, describing her color and markings, for she was actually almost identical to the color of coyotes, telling them not to shoot her. I was so hopeful that she would find her way back to me or we would find her. My dad and I actually went together in his truck, driving all over the area near the man's house, searching and calling for her, but with no luck. And as the days turned to weeks, my hope slipped away that I would ever see her again.

It had been over three weeks with no sighting or report of my dog, and on a Friday night, I had gone to a movie with one of the few people who would still call me friend. It was dark when I got home, and I always entered the garage first and then into the back door of the house. The garage door was on the side of the garage, so the front porch light that was on did little good there. As I opened the door, I was reaching in to turn on a light, but before I got it turned on, something hit me out of the darkness, knocking me onto my back. Fear gave way to inexpressible joy as my attacker began covering my face with licks from her tongue! Yes, she was back! It took her three weeks, and she was very thin, but she was back! It was one of the greatest moments of my life. We rolled around on the ground, me hugging her and her smothering me with kisses. I was laughing so loud my parents finally came to see what was going on, opening up the house door and turning on the garage light. They just watched, and I think maybe, just maybe, it even touched my dad's cold heart, for my dog remained with me for the rest of her life!

Yes, my dad never touched her again, and we never spoke again. For the remainder of my time at home with my parents until the day I graduated from high school and moved away, I never spoke directly to my dad and never made eye contact. Our deepest conversation became "Pass the ketchup." You see, my dad's displeasure with me reached an all-time high after the abortion. He never spoke about it, never once asked me if I was okay. He said nothing. But then he didn't have to; his eyes said everything. In his eyes, I saw hatred, disgust, and disapproval. He treated me like a common whore—not knowing that if ten years before on that night, if he had just picked me up and asked me, "What's wrong?" if he had hugged me and told me everything was going to be okay, if he had just saved me, everything would have been so different. But they weren't, and now at sixteen years old, I hated him more than he hated me.

It's strange, but our hatred for each other started on the night ten years before, when, at six years old, I tried the only way I knew how to get his attention—crying. I was crying out of desperation because I wanted my dad to help me, protect me, save me, but instead of kneeling down and holding me, wondering why his child that was normally very happy would cry this much, beg this much, and all only when brought to this house, he left me. I mean, I just couldn't understand it. There had been a time before we moved to that town when we had been so close. My dad had taken me everywhere with him, even to work. He worked for International Harvester, so he would bring me, and while he was talking to clients and doing his thing, I would play on the shiny new tractors. My dad was a pilot and had a small plane, and he took me flying all the time—even bringing pillows so I could sit in the seat next to him and pretend I was flying! We had so much fun together, laughing all the time, just enjoying being together. And the thing I had loved most about my dad was how he used to sit in a rocking chair with me on his lap and rock me to sleep every night. So why now, when I needed him the most, did he just stand there glaring down at me like I was a spoiled brat just trying to get my way? What happened to us and the love we once shared? Why did he just leave? Leaving me alone with that monster, and now ten years later, I was in the middle of the aftermath of that night.

Ending It

I was doing the best I could, but school was just a constant onslaught. Kids were vicious, and they went out of their way to be cruel to me. I guess it was the pack mentality: when one is down and weak, attack it. And boy did they. Of course, there was "the sister" (my tormenter from that house) who was a year ahead of me and who was always there, running her mouth. Sometime ago, my mom had made me promise not to say anything to her because my dad worked for her dad. "Don't make waves and don't cause trouble for your dad." Like I cared about my dad. But nonetheless, I promised her and I always keep my promises. It just became one more reason for hating my dad because the sister was relentless. She would get her friends together and walk behind me between classes every day and say things like, "Your mom's a whore. Your brothers are worthless. Your dad sleeps with prostitutes. No one in your family will ever amount to anything." It was just never-ending, and the two friends I had left would just look at me, like, "Why don't you say something? Why don't you DO something?" All the while, I kept quiet, never defending myself or my family. But all the while on the inside, I was burning—burning with hatred for her, for her family, for my dad. How desperately I wanted to turn around and beat her to death, silencing that mouth of hers permanently! Oh, how I wanted to take out ALL of my hurt, pain, and anger on her. I had visions of hitting her so hard as to knock her down and then sitting on her chest and pounding her face with my fists until I literally beat her to death. But I didn't, I never broke my promise—not even to this day.

About three months had gone by since the abortion, and I had gone to a movie with my two friends. But I never saw the movie, never heard a word; my mind was being tortured by what I had done.

It was slowly sinking in, the reality of what had happened, what I had done. When I got home, my mom was waiting on the couch in the living room, like she always did when I went out. I said hello and started for my bedroom, but something inside me made me stop and turn around. Something said, "Try one more time to get help from your mom." Desperation was taking over—I needed someone to talk to, someone to help me through all these feelings. So with voice cracking with emotion, I said, "Mom, I need to talk to you about what happened."

She looked me straight in the eyes and said, "Shut up! Quit being a crybaby! As far as I'm concerned, nothing happened, and it will NEVER be spoken about in this house!"

Wow, there it was again! Not a hug, no reassuring words that everything would be okay, no help, no comfort, no "Why did this happen in the first place?" Nothing. Absolutely nothing.

I went to bed and cried myself to sleep. I cried my last tears that night—cried till there was none left. It would be eight long years before I would shed one more tear.

I made it two more months before I could take it no longer, and I decided to kill myself. It would have worked, too, if God had not intervened.

It was summer now, and the darkness had truly won. I had sunk so low into the pit of despair there seemed no way out. Even my beloved horses could not heal this wound. It was simply too deep, too dark, or so I thought. It seemed that every time I tried to climb up and out, something else would come and knock me back down. And with every fall, I went a little deeper. I had tried so hard at first. Just climb—climb your way out of this pit and keep going. But each fall came a little harder and further than the last. I hit the bottom harder and harder, falling further from the top—further from the light. It was much harder to climb out, each time taking longer, and now I found myself so far down I could feel the flames of hell just beneath me. It was so dark and so oppressive I found it hard just to breathe. Now when I looked up, I couldn't see any light at all. I had no more strength to climb. My own thoughts were crushing me. No one seemed to care or even notice the agony I was in. But then by now, I had become really good at appearing normal. Still, I wonder, if anyone would have looked close enough, would they have seen the cracks in my normal?

I had no hope of things being any better or ever changing. I could not shut out my thoughts or shut up that voice in my head. So I decided I would get into my dad's pickup truck and wrap it around a giant light pole. There was a paved road that led to the city park and then out of town to the country. It was mostly flat and very straight. About three miles long, it would end at a T-intersection where gravel roads began. The entrance to the park was just outside of town, and the townspeople had decided it was too dark at the entrance and could be dangerous, so they had a light put in. And it was on the biggest wood post I had ever seen. It was rectangular in shape and multicolored, like a lot of trees pressed together to form this gigantic post. It was perfect, it was huge, and it sat right by the road—no way to miss it!

I got into the truck. It was close to evening; the sun was in the west as I headed for that road. I went down main street, turned left at the corner store and past the co-op over the railroad tracks, and there it was—beautiful to me in all of its giganticness. I drove casually past, left arm out the window, to the end of that paved road. I turned around at the T-intersection, and without hesitation, I slammed my foot down on the gas pedal all the way to the floor. Both my hands were on the wheel now—I could not miss my target. The engine roared, and the white lines became a blur as I screamed toward my goal. I was fast approaching the pole, and I had absolutely no doubt, not a hint of a second thought. In fact, my only thought was, *Don't miss the pole.*

As I neared the point where I needed to turn the wheel to hit that post, something happened right in front of me. Right where the windshield should be, there was a picture—no, more like a movie. Yes, a little movie screen appeared right in front of me, and there she was! The love of my life, my horse Agi Pat! She was moving, moving her head toward me, but it was in slow motion because she was blinking, her eyes closing real slow, and before they opened, it was gone. As soon as the picture was gone, there was a voice. I heard a clear, distinct, audible voice, which said, "Who will take care of her?" The voice was so clear, so real I was just sure someone was sitting next to me.

I jerked my head toward the passenger side, but there was no one there, and as I looked at the empty seat and through the passenger window, I saw the pole, my pole, go by. I turned and looked at the speedometer. I was going ninety-six miles an hour. It would have worked. I took my foot off the accelerator, and as the truck slowed down, my thoughts began to race. The voice was right. Who would take care of her? How could I leave the only one who truly loved me? The only thing on the entire planet that I cared about! The only one who loved me so unconditionally, who was always there for me, who faithfully took me on those long, amazing, life-giving rides. How could I forsake the one who had been saving my life all along? No, I could not, would not, leave her behind. So on that day, I made up my mind that I would stay alive for her sake.

I did not understand at all what just happened. Who actually sent that movie right in front of me. WHOSE voice had just spoken to me. The miracle that was done just for me. Who had really saved my life. No, so dark was the pit I was in all I could see was my own misery. Something I regret to this day is that I did not turn to God right then and there. But I didn't know I could. No one told me I could have a relationship with God himself—that when it seemed no one but a horse loved me, the creator of the entire universe loved me, that I could have turned to him and he would have taken all of my pain and suffering and made it his own, that he would have given me more unconditional love than even Agi Pat could! Oh, the years I have agonized over my decision to stay in the darkness and not turn to the one TRUE light. If only I had followed God on that day instead of the darkness that permeated every aspect of my life. How things would have been so different, all the years of suffering I could have avoided. But I didn't, and now on that day, instead of walking into a new life, free of the pit that I was languishing in, I was faced with a whole new problem—how to stay alive.

Staying Alive

A few weeks had gone by since my attempted suicide, and I was in the barn finishing up chores for the night. I was always in the barn. It was my place of refuge—the only place I felt needed, loved, safe. Periodically, my dad would get drunk and then come out to the barn to harass me. Knowing how much I cared for the horses, he would, for no reason, pick up a shovel, go into one of the stalls, and just start beating a horse. The horse was horrified, knowing it had done nothing wrong. As was I. So I would rush in and get him to turn his attention on me. He would reel around, shovel held like a baseball bat about to be swung, eyes flashing that intense anger and hatred that I had grown accustomed to. And although he never hit me, he would throw the shovel in my direction and storm past me and out of the barn.

It was one such night when Mom had sent Dad to the barn to tell me dinner was ready. I was almost done, just raking the aisle when he came in, drunk and running his mouth. Before he could do anything, I put the rake down, walked to the door, turned off the lights and left. I left him standing in the middle of the barn in the dark, and boy, did it make him furious! Finding his way to the door, he came out and so was about twenty feet behind me as we walked toward the house. The sun was just going down on a beautiful summer night—the beauty destroyed, however, by his drunken ranting. I wasn't really listening, wasn't responding, which only made him madder. That's when he said it—said the words that stopped me dead in my tracks, words that triggered a new level of hatred and unleashed an anger that had been developing for years.

He said, "Hey, little missy, you better watch your step, or you just might come home and find your Agi Pat gone."

Explosions went off in my head. That was it for me. He had just crossed a line! He had just threatened to kill the ONLY reason I was still on planet Earth! Spinning around, I ran straight to him and, face-to-face, eyeball to eyeball, nose to nose, screamed at him, "You miserable bastard! Touch one hair on her body, and you better sleep with one eye open!"

He was completely speechless, and for the first time, I saw something new in his eyes. It wasn't hate; it was fear, and he had good reason to be afraid of me. The one thing my dad had taught me was how to shoot a gun, and like anything I put my mind to, I mastered it. And by that night, at sixteen years old, I was an excellent marksman! I could shoot any type of gun and hit any type of target. So much so that my dad would make bets with his friends about my shooting. He never lost, and I never missed. I freaked out a lot of the guys my dad hung around with who saw me shoot. I was accurate— deadly accurate.

I'm pretty sure my words sobered my dad that night. As he looked into my eyes, he saw the extreme hatred and the absolute truth of what I had said. He wisely took heed of my warning and never touched Agi Pat. In fact, he pretty much stayed out of my way and left me alone from that time on, which suited me just fine.

Deeper and deeper, I sank into the pit of darkness that now enveloped me. Just when I thought I couldn't go any lower, nothing worse could happen, it did. There was no peace, no reprieve. I would just get through one thing, and then something else would happen. And at first, I actually tried to climb out of the pit. Every time I got knocked down, I would get up and climb. Knocked down, get up and climb. But I was getting tired of climbing. I was slowly losing my grip and sinking lower and further from the edge. It was getting harder to get to the top. It seemed so far away now. But I had made the choice to stay alive, and now I had to figure out how to do that. I knew part of that meant I was going to have to climb, but what else? Exactly how does one stay alive when one doesn't want to? The answer? Get drunk.

Yes, lots of beer on Friday and Saturday nights! And I drank A LOT of beer. I was down to one friend, but that was okay because in a town not far from ours, they didn't card her, which meant she could buy us beer! Hallelujah! We would start with a case, twenty-four bottles of Miller Lite. We would play chug-a-lug with all twenty-four, twelve apiece! Once they were gone, we would go to whatever keg party was going on (and there was always a keg party), pay our five dollars, and drink the night away! Drinking became my great escape. I could literally escape into a world where I was happy, a place I could truly laugh where the darkness faded and joy abounded—a place where the boogeyman wasn't real, at least for a little while. But of course, he was, and by Sunday afternoon, as the hangover was wearing off, reality set in. And then Monday morning, I was back to school, back to darkness and being judged constantly. Back to my classmates on one side of the room, me on the other, them laughing and making sure to talk loud enough for me to hear about all the fun they had together—trips to the amusement park, snowmobile parties—making sure I knew I wasn't invited on purpose.

And so high school went. It was EVERY SINGLE day. Oh, but thank God for Friday nights! So this became my new normal—survive the week, make it through till Friday, and then get as drunk as one human being possibly could. It was awesome, and I so loved to get drunk that on Friday I didn't eat lunch or supper just so I could get drunk faster! And remember that ulcer I mentioned earlier? Well, the number one thing you don't do when you have an ulcer is drink beer. So I simply bought a bottle of Maylox and chugged down a few gulps before I started drinking to help with the pain of the hangover. The pain got worse, of course, so I just drank more Maylox. Before long, I was drinking an entire bottle of Maylox to cope with the pain. It was awful, though. The pain was so horrible and so intense my stomach felt like it was on fire. It was excruciating and so completely worth it. So worth a few hours of laughter and happiness, a few hours of freedom from the darkness, and a few hours of feeling okay with me.

So that's how I did it—that's how I stayed alive. Drink until you pass out 'cause while you're drunk, life is good, and when you're passed out, you feel nothing. Awesome. The only thing about not wanting to be alive, though, is, you don't care, and being a very type-A person, I pushed everything to the extreme. When I worked, I worked really hard, and oh yes, when I played, I played even harder. I took everything to the extreme. When I drank, I drank way more than I should. When I drove (drunk), I drove way faster than I should. Yes, I drove drunk—drove like the wind! And when you have a Firebird with a 401 four-barrel, you really can fly! The speedometer on my car went to one hundred forty miles per hour, and I was always maxing it out and pushing the needle past the one hundred forty mark while completely drunk! I did things like race down gravel roads. Yeah, I knew a guy that was always at the same keg parties as me. He drove a Trans-Am. When it was time to leave, we would get into our cars and then race the five or six miles to the highway side by side—me on the wrong side of the road, racing on gravel and over hills, doing ninety-five miles an hour. And did I mention we were on gravel? When we reached the highway, he would turn right to go to his town, and I would turn left, and then it was full speed ahead to my town! My one friend who stayed with me was herself a bit of a rebel and an outcast also. She could buy beer, which was awesome, and was the only one brave enough to get in the car with me for the ride home! Most nights I drove, but there were those times I was just too drunk. Barely able to walk, my friend would drag me back to the car, stumbling and falling the whole way because she, of course, was completely drunk too.

Finally, the day of graduation had come! It was the day of my release, like a prisoner being set free, and the greatest day of my life! *Free at last. Free at last. Thank God Almighty I'm free at last!* Or so I thought.

I left immediately—left those classmates, left that family, left my family—and I moved to Ohio and took a job on a large and prestigious horse farm. This is all I had ever wanted—to train horses and compete on a national level—and here I was working on one of the biggest and most nationally known horse farms in the country! I worked hard, and within one month, I went from being a groom to being the assistant trainer! *All right! I'm here! I've made it and am living the dream! Life just got a whole lot better!* Now I would put behind me all those things that happened, all that ugliness, because you know, if you don't talk about something, don't speak it out loud, then it never really happened. At least, that's how I reasoned things out. Just don't talk about it, and then it's like it never really happened. I had new friends now and a whole new life, so things should be different, right? But somehow the darkness found me. Somehow it had followed me, all those miles away. But not to worry; my new friends liked to get drunk, too, so I could still get drunk on the weekends and at least I'm away from that family.

New Life?

Things were great at first. The trainer, who was my hero, and I got along great! She seemed to really like me, and of course, I thought she was it! She was everything I wanted to be—manager of a huge horse farm with forty-five horses in training over a hundred horses on the farm and very successful in the show arena. I mean, this was it, and I was exactly where I wanted to be!

The owner of the farm, who is also a trainer, was nice to me at first, but then he started becoming very verbally abusive and incredibly hard on me—more so than anyone else who worked there. Even the trainer was shocked. She couldn't believe how he treated me and kept saying, "I don't know why he is treating you like that." It was horrible, I'm finally where I want to be and, this guy is going out of his way to make my life miserable. He said shocking things to me. I was only eighteen years old, and it was disturbing to me. This guy didn't know just how stubborn a redhead from Nebraska could be. No one was going to chase me away from my own dream! And besides, where was I going to go? Certainly not back to that town with that family and my family. No, this guy might be a jerk, but it was way better than what I left, so I did not quit.

I just got up every morning, worked really hard every day, and got drunk every weekend! Yes, you can handle anything during the week because another weekend is coming! It worked all through high school, right? Why would this be any different? It was a new life but the same pattern, but at least, I was training horses, and really that's all that mattered to me. I mean, as long as there are horses in my life, I would be okay, right? I mean, that's just how it is. Life is hard. Bad things always happen. Everyone goes through what I've gone through, so I just got to put up with whatever I have got to put up with. So long as I can train horses, who cares about people, anyway? They mean nothing to me. You certainly can't trust them, can't count on them for anything except to hurt you, so my great revelation of life is that I decided humans are just something that have to be tolerated. Some of them weren't so bad—at least, not the ones who like to get drunk like I did, so that was cool. Get drunk with them but don't let them in. Into your real world, where you would actually like to be friends with them, share things with them, count on them to be there for you. No, just keep them at arm's length, get drunk with them, work with them, but never ever let them in. So that's what I did, and I actually got really good at it. Maybe too good. That's just how I am.

When I make up my mind about something, I go after it with everything I have. Pursue it relentlessly. Do whatever is necessary, work as hard as you got to until you master it. Like I said before, very type A. I'm not one for sitting around. Besides, you sit around too much, and all you can hear is that voice—the one that keeps telling you how bad you are, that you're worthless, that you will never amount to anything and will never be anything but a failure. No, no, better to stay busy. Funny how that voice became my slave driver. I figured if I could just work hard enough, push myself more, that would make me feel better about myself. No matter how much I worked, no matter how hard I push myself (by age eleven, I was getting up at four in the morning and working horses before school and then coming home and working horses after school), it just never seemed to be enough; the voice was never satisfied.

So things went along on the horse farm, and over time, the owner started being nice to me, and we actually started getting along really well! I'm not exactly sure what changed, but I think it all had been a test. I think this guy wanted to make sure I was tough enough to make it in the horse world.

A couple years after I had started, he told me, "You know, Janel, you have a lot of talent with horses. But it takes more than talent to survive in this business. You've got to have thick skin, be just plain old tough, and you've got to have money behind you, or you will not survive in this business." That's a lot of wisdom to lay on a twenty-year-old. And of course, in my youthfulness, I thought, *Don't worry, old man (he was probably forty at the time), I got this!* not knowing just how true those words would prove to be and how wise that man really was.

Fixing Them—Fixing Me

A shift had started on that horse farm. I, as the assistant trainer, was given what everyone called the second-string horses. The trainer, of course, worked the first-string horses, but I never looked at these horses like they were second best, and I certainly never told them that. I knew that every horse was special in their own way and that every horse—if given a chance—would go on to do great things, whatever that might be. Besides, I hated labels. People were always putting labels on me—wrong labels. They didn't know me, and worse yet, they didn't even try! They NEVER looked inside, never tried to see what was really going on. No, I hated labels and I would not do that to the horses I loved, and by the way, I loved them all.

So I started training the so called "second-string" horses. Who actually had been with another trainer previously, who had abused them terribly. For those of you who don't know horses, abused horses are ANGRY—REALLY ANGRY! And at twelve hundred pounds of solid muscle, they are really good at making their opinions known! They are extremely dangerous, volatile, and unpredictable. If they can't buck you off, they run you into walls, smashing your legs and trying to knock you off. If you turn your back on them, they will bite you, and horses have over five hundred pounds per square inch of force when they bite. A big dog has two hundred pounds per square inch. Horses can snap your bones like a toothpick; you definitely don't want to ever be bitten by a horse. Beyond biting, if they can, they will get you down on the ground and strike and stomp you with fatal bone-crushing blows from their hard feet.

Needless to say, working around these kinds of horses comes with unique challenges and great risks. Nothing about that ever bothered me, though. I was never scared or intimidated by these horses because I knew exactly where it was coming from. It was never personal, they were just mad—mad at life, mad at people who hurt them for no reason, and mad that their lives are so hard—and they didn't understand why, so they dropped into survival mode and did whatever was necessary just to stay alive. I saw through all their anger, all their antics. However dangerous and dramatic they were, these were not bad horses like everyone wanted to label them. They were simply broken horses. My heart was broken for them for what had happened to them, what they had been through, and I was going to fix them—not knowing that I was really trying to fix myself and not understanding that I was just as broken as they were.

You see, I didn't see myself as broken. I didn't see myself as abused because I truly believed this stuff happens to everyone. This was just life, so deal with it. So a very broken girl started working some very broken horses, and our journey together began. I worked with these horses through the fall and all winter, and by spring, I had a string of beautiful horses who were more than ready to go show the world what they had accomplished! Their transformations were amazing, although if you looked closely, you could still see some residue from their former abuse. Mostly they were changed, and I could not wait to show them.

The owner and the trainer agreed that I should show these horses since I had been working them but were secretly thinking that I would fall flat on my face and that these horses were never going to go out and show like she said they would. We knew they couldn't; they were just second-string horses, anyway. I was resolute in my thinking, though. I knew these horses would never let me down. I knew that horses—these horses—are, by nature, very noble, loyal, and fearless companions. It's just in their nature to be great. They can't help themselves, it's just in their DNA. They were simply created to be amazing creatures! The only real problem horses have is the people around them. Horses cannot help who owns them or who will train them. And if they fall into the wrong hands, if the people around them are mean and abusive, they go from amazing, loving creatures to fearful, angry ones, and most of them never reach their full potential. They never get to be exactly who and what they were supposed to be, never get to be brave when someone is scared, never get to be strong when someone is weak, never get to shower unconditional love on a very broken human.

Oh. Wow. Could the very same thing be said about children? Is not every child born with something special in them? Does not every human have the capacity to do something great? Okay, wow, that is way too deep for me. I mean, at the time, I was exactly like these horses—I had dropped into survival mode, doing whatever I could to survive.

So my first show with these horses was now only a few days away. I was beyond excited and I just couldn't wait! So what to do to blow off some nerves and anticipation? Play football, of course. Oh yes, I'm a huge football fan and I loved to play it and watch it! It was wonderful, and I could hit people as hard as I wanted and not get in trouble! And oh boy, did I hit them—every tackle was just a little more of that anger coming out. It was almost as good as getting drunk! I could hit them with incredible force, which was shocking to the people I played against. They had no idea that a hundred ten pounds could hit so hard. They had no clue that every time I smashed them into the ground, I was smashing pent-up anger, resentment, fear, betrayal. It was intoxicating to me. Completely renewing, it was a few brief moments of me being in charge of my life and being in control and of me inflicting the pain. But unfortunately, this game would not end well for me.

After a punishing game, we had come down to the final play. They gave me the ball, and I scored the winning touchdown. One of the guys we were playing against (it was girls against guys) did not enjoy losing to us and stormed into the end zone and hit me from behind so hard he snapped my right leg. *Pop!* It was loud, like a gun had gone off, and then it was all over. All my work all winter gone in a single second. My leg was badly broken, and there would be no walking and certainly no riding for several weeks. I was so close to my dream, and then someone took it from me. And just like that, just when I thought I had gotten myself out of that damn pit of darkness, I slid right back to the very bottom.

It was a long fall, and I landed hard. It knocked the breath out of me, and I lay there for a moment, thinking of all the times I had spent at the bottom of this pit, how many times I got up and started climbing, and how tired I was of climbing. But being only twenty years old, I thought that this was okay. *All right, I got this and I can get outta here.* So I got right up and started climbing.

The trainer took one of the horses I had worked with—he was a little red stallion. After many trials and tribulations, he had excelled at his work, and he was the one I was most excited to show! So the trainer rode him once at home, took him to the show, and proceeded to win every class that she went in with him. Then he ended up being the Open Park Saddle Champion of the whole show. In the Morgan world, there is nothing more important or prestigious than winning the Open Park Saddle class. My little guy had done it! He had overcome the hardships, the labels, the abuse and showed everyone just how great he is!

Of course, I was proud of him, but I was also very sad—sad that I had worked so hard all winter, sad that I had believed in him when no one else did, sad that I did not get to share the moment of his victory with him. It might be a longer climb out of this pit than I thought.

So the trainer got home from the show, and I was thinking, *All right, at least, she will be happy with me. I should at the very least get a "Thank you" or "Good job" from her.* She walked into the trailer house where we lived. I was on the couch with my leg propped up on pillows.

She sat down at the kitchen table and said to me, "Come here."

I got my crutches and hobbled over to sit next to her. She had a big manila envelope with her. She opened it and pulled out a picture. The picture was of her and my little guy making their victory pass. She laid it on the table in front of me, and there he was, my beautiful red stallion doing his thing! It was breathtaking! Thinking she was about to give me a compliment (now remember in that picture this was only the third time she had ever sat on his back), I waited with eager anticipation! But then she pointed to his knee. In a park class, the horse has to be able to pick his knee and foot up really high up even with his chest, which, by the way, is incredibly hard, and only a few horses can do it. They are considered the elite athletes of the horse world. Like a Michael Jordan, if you will. I was still waiting to hear what she would say, and this was what I heard.

"Do you see that?"

"Yes," I said.

She asked again, "Do you see that?"

Again, I answered yes. She was tapping her finger now on the picture at his knee, and she said, "Do you see all that trot?"

"Yes." I nodded.

"You see all that trot right there? It's all because of me, and don't you EVER forget it!"

It was like being hit in the face with a two-by-four that I never saw coming. It happened again—the one person I looked up to, the one person I thought I could depend on and trust, the one I thought believed in me, my hero, had just turned on me like everyone else in my life!

Yup, my pit just got a little deeper and a little darker. I eventually healed and returned to showing, and I was becoming very successful. It was great being out of the pit and doing exactly what I was created to do! My success continued right up to the point of whenever I showed against my boss and one-time hero, I was beating her. Needless to say, that went over real well, and things quickly deteriorated between us—to the point I finally had to quit.

Funny, on the day I left, the owner, who had once been so abusive to me, stood before me with tears in his eyes as we said our goodbyes. By now, the two of us had grown quite close to each other. Well, as close as I could safely allow. But nonetheless, we hugged and cried. I cried—I was actually going to miss this guy. Somewhere along the way, he had become really important to me. Unfortunately for me, I did not know that this would be the last time I would ever see him. Ever. And what about my one-time hero? Well there would be no hug from her—or even a goodbye.

Deadly Betrayal

So here I was back in Nebraska and exactly one block from that house again, which was completely unacceptable, and I had no intention of staying. So I called a friend who also showed Morgan's. She lived about seventy-five miles from me. I asked her if I could come stay with her for a while, just until I figure out where to go next. She said yes, and I agreed to feed and clean stalls for her in exchange for living with her and her family. She was older than me and was married with two teenage kids. She didn't pay me anything, just gave me a place to live and fed me.

While I was staying with her, one of the kids I had gone to school with found out I was back in Nebraska and that she lived only a few miles away in a larger city. At one time in my life, this girl and I had been friends—best friends. We met in sixth grade and quickly became inseparable. She was the one who had taken me to that party and then the one who had introduced me to beer. But of course, she had become one of the gang that had turned on me and treated me as an outcast. But it's many years later, and I thought maybe she's changed. *Maybe I've changed—maybe it's just easier to forgive and forget? Who knows, maybe she actually feels bad and wants to try and make things right?* I didn't know, but when she called me and asked if I wanted to get together, I said yes. She told me to "bring some extra clothes and just spend the night here with me and drive back on Sunday." It sounded good, so Saturday morning, I was up at six to do all the chores, clean all the stalls, and work all the horses. I did the evening chores, showered, and headed to town.

When I got there, we just kind of picked right up like nothing had happened and we had always been friends. We were sitting there, trying to decide what to do when another old classmate showed up.

So we decided that all three of us—me, her, and him—would go to a club to drink and dance. But by now, I had a full-blown bleeding ulcer, and I told them I wasn't going to drink. The pain had just become too much, so I told them I would be the designated driver and they could drink all they wanted.

At the end of the night (in Nebraska at that time, the bars closed at midnight), we were walking to the car, but now a second guy was walking with us, and my friend asked if it was okay to give him a ride back to his apartment. Sure, I didn't care, figuring he lived at the same complex. When we got there and got out the car, my friend stopped and turned to me and said, "I thought you said you would give him a ride home."

I said, "I just did."

She said, "Well, he doesn't live here. He lives a few blocks away."

"Great! He can walk home."

But she insisted. "Please give him a ride to his apartment."

Well, it finally dawned on me that she wanted to sleep with the other guy and I would only be in the way. "Okay, fine, I will drive him down the block." Of course, it took like one minute to get to his place, so to kill a little time, we sat and talked. But I was tired; I'd been up working all day, and I wanted to go to bed. But he was, like, "Come on into my apartment. You can have a Pepsi. We can watch a little TV. You know, you have to give them some time." Ugh. He was right, even though I was really tired, I did not want to walk in on them. So I finally relented and went up to his third-story apartment. I had my Pepsi, watched a little TV, and then got up to leave. The apartment was little, so I sat at the end of the couch near the door. There was a long coffee table in front of the couch, which I walked around to get to the door.

With my back to the door, I looked at him and asked him where I should put my glass. He stood up and walked toward me. Thinking he was going to take the glass, I held it out toward him. He just walked by. I thought, *Okay, well, he is going to get the door for me,* so I bent over and set the glass on the coffee table. Then I stood up, but before I could turn toward the door, he grabbed me by the neck with one of his arms and proceeded to pick me up off the floor by my neck. This guy was about six feet four, 220 pounds, and a worked-out-every-day kind of guy. Then he said, "You ain't going anywhere, bitch!" and then I heard him lock all three locks he had on his door.

My first thought was, *This is not happening.* My second thought was, *I'm not going to let this happen, and the fight was on.* I didn't really understand what was going on and why this was happening, why only a minute before this guy was laughing and friendly but not now. Now in an instant, I was in a fight for my life. He had me by my neck, walking toward the hallway. Now I had never been in this apartment before or down that hallway, but I knew exactly where that hallway led to—the bedroom. I knew exactly what would happen in that bedroom. With great resolve, I made up my mind: I WOULD NOT GO DOWN THAT HALLWAY!

As he approached the opening to the hall, I put my feet up, one on each side, and pushed as hard as I could. Surprising my attacker, we both launched backwards, crashing into a table with a lamp on it. The lamp went flying, breaking the light bulb and landing on the table. We smashed it to pieces. We rolled around on the ground for a moment. I frantically pulled at his arm around my neck but to no avail. He was simply too strong, so I went for his eyes as best I could, reaching behind me, but he was able to deflect me with his other hand. He was struggling to get back on his feet, which he did, but he stood up right by the hallway again, and without hesitating, I launched us again. I pushed as hard as my adrenaline-seized body could.

Upending us both again, he landed squarely on his back. I again tried to pull his arm from my neck. I was desperate now, my lungs burning for the air they so desperately needed! I was fighting, squirming, and unable to yell for help, I just kept fighting. I remember so clearly that I was staring at the ceiling and how the panels looked, to this day I remember how those panels looked. That would be the last thing I remembered as I lost consciousness.

When I opened my eyes again, it was dark, and I wasn't on top of him anymore. He was on top of me, raping me. My clothes were gone, my strength was gone, but I was still going to fight with what little energy I could muster. I took a swing and punched him in the side of his head. It wasn't enough to hurt him, only piss him off, and this time, he got my neck with both hands and, shaking as he choked me, said, "I'm going to fuck you dead or alive, bitch."

I had my hands on his, trying so hard to loosen his grip. My lungs were burning so bad I felt as if they were on fire inside my chest. My eyes were bulging out of my head, like they might explode! And then out of nowhere, I saw it—saw this beautiful sunset, like something you would see in Hawaii, and then there was my brother Randy, and he was laughing, but it was in slow motion because he blinked real slow, and before his eyes could open, it was gone. And in the darkness, a realization came over me. I knew two things in that moment: I knew I wasn't going to see the sun come up and that I would never see my family again. I was dying. In that instant, even though all of my life I had wanted to die, in that bedroom, in that apartment, on that night, I wanted to live.

I made the decision to live, so I let go of his hands, let my arms fall down and out to the side, and lay very, very still. I played dead. He didn't let go right away, though. This time, he wanted to make sure I was dead—there would be no waking up on him again.

There are no words to describe how hard it was to just lie there, pretending that you didn't need air, and how hard it was, when he finally did loosen his grip a little on my neck, not to just gulp in the air that my body so desperately needed and wanted. What it was like to take in little tiny breaths of air, so small that they would go unde-tected by the one hand he kept on my neck, while he went back to raping me. What it was like to play dead while he raped me over and over for hours! Thirty years later and my whole body still shudders at just trying to write this book.

After several hours, he eventually fell asleep, and I started inch-ing my way toward the edge of the bed. When I finally made it to the edge, the sun was coming up, and light started filling the room. I could see my pants on the floor and my shirt beside them. I pains-takingly, slowly got off the bed, got to my clothes, and pulled on my pants and shirt. I started to creep down that hall, which had a wooden floor, and partway down it, it creaked under my weight.

I froze. I heard him rustle a little in the bed, and then he resumed his heavy breathing. I continued down the hall. When I got back into the little living room area, I saw the broken tables and lamps and the knocked-over chairs, the evidence of the struggle that took place. Then I saw my purse, still on the floor by the door. I quickly but quietly moved to it and started to unlock those three locks. The chain was easy, but the dead bolt opened with a loud clunk. And yes, it was so loud it woke him up. He started yelling because, remember, he thought I was dead and now I was about to escape and he couldn't let that happen! No way he was going to let me go and tell what he had just done to me.

I struggled with the last lock—it was one of those twisting doorknob locks that I hate to this very day! They never unlock easy or in the same way twice, who makes these things anyway?. I was in full panic mode now and I was twisting and turning that damn knob every which way, and just as he burst out of the hall into the living room, it opened! I threw back the door and ran barefoot toward the staircase. I flew down those three flights of stairs and hit the door at the bottom at full speed. The door, the doorframe, and I crashed out onto the sidewalk!

I got up and started running. I had no idea where I was at or where my car was parked. I was too panicked to think right! I don't know but I think I ran all the way around the building before finding my car. The only thing I do remember about then is how bright the sun was that morning, how white the walls of that apartment building were, and that the capital building looked so big as I was running. Funny how the mind works and what you remember in moments like that.

Finally, I found my car and got in and got going, but where would I go? Still not thinking clearly, I decided to go back to my friend's house and get my stuff and go home. I knocked on her door early that Sunday morning, and I was shocked at what she said to me! She opened the door, took one look at me, and said, "Wow, looks like someone had fun last night."

What? Are you kidding me? Do I look like I had fun? Now I hadn't seen myself yet, but I was pretty sure I did not look like I had had fun. Brushing past her, I gathered my stuff and left. I drove home, crept in quietly so as not to wake the family I was staying with, and went into the bathroom, having decided I would take a hot shower and try to wash off what had just happened to me.

That was when I first saw myself. I looked in the mirror and did not recognize who, or maybe I should say what, was looking back at me. My hair was wild and tangled. The whites of my eyes were bright red like a vampire or something. My neck was purple and red with bruises. My eyes were so creepy I scared myself. I had to quit looking.

I took a long hot shower and then spent the day in bed. By the end of the day, the people I was staying with were worried about me, as I was still in bed, so I faked having a cold and told them I was just too sick to get up.

The next morning, Monday, I got up to go to work as if nothing had happened and was shocked that my eyes were still bright red, so I coughed a lot and told everyone I must have coughed so hard that I broke the blood vessels in my eyes. It worked; they seemed satisfied. But I was more shocked when I tried to speak. My voice was virtually gone. It was hoarse and raspy, which only lended more credit to my story of having a cold. As for my neck, I simply wore turtlenecks, as it was still chilly out. But I quickly realized my neck was hurt far worse than I thought. Not only could I not talk, but I was also unable to swallow food. I was barely able to swallow anything! It was so painful I didn't eat solid food for several months. I lived on broth and Diet Coke.

The next several days and nights were extremely hard. The days were not as bad, as I was able to focus on the horses. Working horses always had been, would always be, my saving grace. There was just something about them—how they could draw you into their world, a world where there is no judging, no lying, no betraying. Horses are absolute in their honesty and behavior. They always live in the moment, able to forgive quickly, love completely. I always felt a little bit better about myself when I was around them, and feeling good about me was in short supply these days, especially since the attack.

At night, alone with my thoughts and feelings, a new darkness was creeping in. The why of it was taking over. Why had I gone to his apartment? Why had I turned my back on him? Why had I let this happen? *Of course, it was my fault,* I reasoned. *I mean, I was the one who went there, let my guard down, trusting her, trusting him. Idiot. Oh my god, if you weren't so stupid, weren't so weak, it would never have happened!*

As self-hatred started to take over me, so did feelings of help-lessness, shame, and regret on a whole new level. He took a great deal from me, stripping me of any security I might have had—the way I was completely helpless to do anything to stop it, feelings of absolute power and control he had over me, my life! No, living with all these thoughts, emotions, and now nightmares of the attack was devastat-ing, and I hated myself for not fighting to the death. I hated myself for still being alive. Regret wracked my mind and overwhelmed my thoughts, and a new resolve rose up in me. Never again would some-thing like this happen to me. Never again would I be somebody's victim. Oh no, no, next time, I would absolutely fight to the death. Theirs or mine didn't matter—I just knew I would never live with these kinds of feelings again.

As I said, I got up Monday and went to work like nothing had happened, like I had not just been in a fight for my very life, had not been raped again, and had not once again stared death in the face. And then once again—just as I was about to die—there had been that little movie screen right in front of me, just like the one of my horse on the day I tried to kill myself, the one of the sunset and my brother. I didn't even know what it was at the time, and I didn't really care. All I knew is that the little movie in front of me once again made me choose to stay alive, and now once again I find myself in a horrible situation and didn't know what to do.

I did know one thing, though—don't go to the cops. They wouldn't believe me, anyway. I mean, why would they? When my own family never believed me, never helped me, never did anything, why would complete strangers? No, better to keep it to myself.

That Monday was agonizing. My throat hurt, my mind was racing, and I did not know how to process what had just happened to me. I didn't know what to do, what to say, what to feel. I really, needed someone to talk to. I really wanted to talk to my mom, and after mulling it over and over in my head, I decided I would call her and try one more time to get help from her.

It was the end of the day, and the woman I was staying with said, "Let's go watch the five-o'clock news and have a Diet Coke." So we all agreed and headed for the house. I was thinking, *Yes, I will sit for a little bit. I'm really tired, and a cold Coke might soothe my burning throat a little. I'll watch the news and then call my mom.* Remember that this is before cellphones, which meant I would have had to use the phone in the kitchen and hope everyone would stay down in the family room watching TV and that no one would overhear what I would be saying.

We sat down just in time for the five o'clock news, and the first thing we hear was, "Breaking news, a small-town bank is closed, and the vice president, has been arrested!" They were putting handcuffs on my dad, he was the vice president, and as they were leading him away, the camera panned wide, and there was my mom watching as they took her husband, following him as they led him away. So much for calling Mom now. She had trouble enough of her own.

The woman in whose home I was staying at, the one who was supposed to be my friend, said with a great deal of sarcasm, "I didn't know we knew a celebrity." Thanks. Thanks for reassuring me everything would be okay. Surely it was a mistake. Thanks for comforting me in a tough situation. Thanks!

In an instant, all these things flashed through my mind, on top of it all the thoughts of the rape, the fight, the struggle just to be alive—how only two nights before I had almost become just another statistic. All these thoughts swirled together so fast in my mind I became dizzy. Things, thoughts, feelings, emotions—they all blurred together. It was just too much, too fast, and then shut down—my mind just seemed to stop for just a moment, and then there was only this thought: *Thanks, bitch!*

I got up and left the room in silence. As I was leaving, I heard her husband say, "Why would you say something like that?"

I retreated to my room, left alone again with all these thoughts, feelings, and emotions that I didn't know what to do with, how to process, or how to understand. All I knew was that the weight of those thoughts pushed me deeper—a lot deeper into the darkness. There, alone in that room, I slid even deeper into the pit of despair that had completely engulfed my life. The light at the top of this pit had now become just a small speck, barely visible to the naked eye. And over the following weeks, with the reality of living with having gone through such a brutal attack, the light disappeared altogether as deeper and deeper I sank.

While trying to sort out and deal with the multitudes of feelings and thoughts of the attack, my reality had changed in another way. When they arrested my dad, they also froze our accounts, which meant I had no money. Not only did they freeze them, they actually took them. They also took all of my dad's retirement that he had saved. He was fifty-nine years old when this happened. Took all the money in the four accounts he had for each of his children. They took our home, our land, our horses, everything. They took it, and why? Guilty by association. After much investigating and a trial, they could find nothing against my dad. What they did find was that his brother-in-law, my uncle, was guilty. He was the president of the bank where they worked together, and he stole money from the bank, from widows, from anyone he could, and he laundered it through Vegas. And because my dad knew him and worked for him, even though they could find no wrongdoing of my dad, they destroyed him for simply knowing him. They took everything from us. As if that family had not already taken enough from me, now they had brought down the whole family.

Though as the dust settled and the local people—our friends— realized that my dad had done nothing wrong, they offered him his job back at the bank. In fact, large banks in larger cities offered him jobs at their banks as well. But unfortunately, it was too late. For you see, they hadn't just taken away our money and our possessions, no, they had taken something far greater. They took away my dad's self-esteem, confidence, and the one thing Dad valued over every other thing—his word. Dad was the kind of man who didn't need a signature on a piece of paper. No, if my dad shook your hand and looked you in the eyes and said he was going to do something, then that was that. No signature, no piece of paper could carry the weight of my dad's word. And everyone in the community knew it! No, this was the man who would run into the local grocery store, grab a loaf of bread and a gallon of milk, and hold it up and yell, "Hey, Marvin, this is what I got," and Marvin would yell back, "Okay, Norm," and away my dad would go. He didn't have to stand in the checkout line. He didn't have to pay right at that moment. No, Marvin knew—like everyone else in town—Norm's good for it.

My dad always came back and paid for it when there was no line, of course, because, you see, my dad was busy. He was busy working in the bank, but more importantly, he was busy helping other people, busy taking care of his place. When it snowed, he was up early on his little Ford tractor—coveralls over his suit and tie—cleaning driveways for the elderly people in town. At lunch, you might find him on that same Ford tractor, scrapping horse manure out of a pen! This was the way of my dad—working, helping, and keeping his word. But now, he felt the trust had been broken—that his word, his honor, his integrity would always be questioned, and that was simply too much for my dad to bear. And the weight of his thoughts crushed him, and he would never truly get up from this again. Oh yes, to some of those around him, he seemed to recover, but to us, his family, we knew otherwise.

A couple weeks had passed since that night of the attack, and I received a phone call from the girl I was supposed to have spent the night with. She said, "I haven't heard from you, and there's something I need to talk to you about," so I agreed to meet her at Village Inn. She had offered to buy me lunch, as she had heard about the bank closing. So I went. I decided I should probably warn her about the guy who attacked me—warn her not to hang out with him.

So we were sitting there, waiting for our lunch, and I started telling her that I didn't think it was safe for her to be around this guy, but before I could tell her why, she dropped a bombshell. Interrupting me, she told me how this guy had raped her and how she had become pregnant. And when she told him she was pregnant, he demanded that she have an abortion. She told him she wouldn't, and he proceeded to beat her so badly she ended up in the hospital and lost the baby.

Wait a minute. Hold on. Let me get my head around this. You're telling me you knew this guy was a rapist, violent, and capable of hurting someone, and you ASKED ME TO GIVE HIM A RIDE HOME? AND YOU ARE SUPPOSED TO BE MY FRIEND? No, no, no, no, no, no, no, this cannot be happening. I did not just hear you say that. You could not have done that to me! I trusted you! Why! Why would you do this to me?

I was speechless. Again my head was swimming, drowning in all these thoughts as one horrifying realization after another crashed in on me. I was there to help her, warn her, protect her for God's sake! And she knowingly—very much on purpose—put me in harm's way, knowing full well that he would rape me! A sick feeling came over me as I realized she knew that he was dangerous and capable of hurting people! And not only that, but she also continued to hang out with him!

Nope, overloaded again. My mind just could not process this and simply shut down, leaving me with only one thought: *F——you, you f——ing bitch!* And without a word, I got up and left. I never looked back, never called her. In fact, that was the last time I ever saw her.

Starting Over

Life went on, and my family and I were struggling to come to grip with our new reality. We were desperate to come up with some money just so we could buy food and keep going. So we had a sale and sold whatever things we had left—couches, TV, etc. Everything sold, at the time, I didn't realize it, but looking back, I believe the townspeople came together and bought everything to help us in the only way they knew how.

Mom gave me fifteen hundred dollars and told me to move back to Ohio and try to get work out there. So that was what I did. I called a friend of mine who was leasing a barn, and we decided we would train together and try to get a business started. I had two horses that were very nice and convinced the IRS not to take them to a sale but let me take them with me and sell them for more money. They agreed. So I took my cat, my dog, the clothes I had left, and the two horses—a mare and a stallion—and left for Ohio.

My brother rode with me to make sure I got there okay and would take a bus back. Now remember, I had fifteen hundred dollars, and that was it, with which I had to buy gas to get to Ohio and then live on until I could get a job. We made it to a toll booth just outside of Chicago, and when we went to pull up, the truck just quit. It would not move. We had to call a tow truck—fifty dollars—to tow us to a little town with a Chevy dealer. He took us to their parking lot and then left. It was Sunday evening—they opened at seven the next morning. I had a cat, a dog, and two horses that needed food and water.

Not knowing what to do, I walked across the street to a restaurant and used the pay phone to call my friend and tell her I wouldn't be there tonight and that I was not sure when I would get there.

When I hung up, there was a man standing there. Thinking he was waiting for the phone, I headed for the door. He stopped me and asked, "Are you the one with the truck an' trailer that was towed in?"

"Yes," I answered.

"Are there horses on that trailer?"

"Yes," I answered.

"Do you have anywhere to put them?"

"No."

Then he told me, "I have horses, and I can call where I keep them and see if you can get a couple stalls for the night."

"Wow, that would be great," I said but thinking to myself, *How much is this going to cost? And I'm going to have to pay another tow fee.* I sank a little further into the darkness. He made a call, and the owner of the stable agreed to take the horses and said it would be ten dollars apiece for the night. *Whew! That is a relief—it's going to cost another fifty dollars for the tow and twenty for the night, but at least my horses will be safe and well cared for.*

The tow truck brought us back to the dealership—we were able to leave the trailer at the farm. So my brother and I, along with my cat and dog, slept in the truck overnight. The next morning, the dealership pulled our truck in to the shop to see what was wrong with it. After a little while, they came to the waiting room and told us the timing chain was broken and that it would be fifteen hundred dollars to fix it.

My heart just sank—as did my brother's. We were both numb and, not knowing what to do, told them to just give us a minute to think about this. They said okay and then left. It was just my brother and I in the waiting room, just sitting there in silence, unsure of what to do. We didn't have enough to pay them. I only had fifteen hundred to start with, and now we'd used some for gas and one hundred on tow fees!

There, in the silence of that little waiting area, I sank ever deeper into the darkness of what seemed to be a bottomless pit. It was at that very moment when the door of that little waiting area opened, and as it did, sunshine spilled into the room, and with the sunshine came that man—the man who had found us stalls for the horses and who had driven out to the barn with us to show us the way and helped us find the right stalls, making sure the horses were okay. The man, who was a complete stranger that was helping us for no reason, was now standing in the doorway. I remember he was a big man filling that door, and yet I don't remember his name.

He stepped in, and as the door swung shut, darkness filled the room once again. He had come to find out what was wrong with the truck. We told him and what it would cost, and he said, "I have a friend that's a mechanic. Let me call him and see what he says." He left for a moment, and when he returned, he told us his friend said he would fix our truck for seven hundred and fifty dollars and that he could do it right away.

A sense of relief washed over me as I thought, *Well, at least, I can make it to Ohio now.*

We called the tow truck again, and off we went to another garage. After the mechanic looked at the truck, he said it would take him all day to fix it and that we could pick it up in the morning. Now we needed somewhere to put my very large dog and cat, so once again, stranger to the rescue! He found a cheap motel for us and the cat, and then he drove us and my dog to his house where he had a large kennel outside that he wasn't using. It was great; it had a large doghouse attached to a large enclosed run. And so with my animals safe, I was once again relieved. This stranger then drove us out to check on the horses and then back to town and bought us lunch!

Early the next morning, this man, this amazing man, was at our hotel with my dog, ready to take us to our truck! Off we went to get our truck and head for the barn, the stranger in the lead, of course! We hooked the trailer, loaded the horses, and thanked our newfound friend over and over, and with that, we were back on the road to Ohio.

By the time we got there, there wasn't much left of the fifteen hundred I started with. I took the first job I could get, and that was working at a fast food restaurant that was open twenty-four hours. I worked the ten-at-night-to-seven-in-the-morning shift, so I was able to work horses during the day. That one job was not enough, though, to cover horse feed, hay, and shavings, as well as food for me, my dog, and my cat, so I started a second job at a greenhouse, 2:00 p.m. to 6:00 p.m. I worked three jobs—Hardee's all night, slept a couple hours, got up, worked the horses, then be at the greenhouse by two till six, and then Hardee's by seven.

Horses, however, are expensive, and I struggled to keep us all fed. So I devised a way to take the hamburgers that were supposed to be thrown away. Once they had sat for a certain time, they had to be thrown out, so I would pretend to throw them away but instead stuff them into my pants' pockets. I would then excuse myself to use the restroom, where I would put them in my purse so I could take them home with me. This was what I lived on—expired hamburgers. My animals never went hungry.

This was how I lived for over a year when I received a phone call from someone looking for a horse trainer. He offered me a place to live for free and seven hundred fifty dollars a month. I thought I had died and gone to heaven. I accepted, packed up the horses, dog, and cat, and away I went, thinking my luck had changed. As I settled into my new job, I was excited. Things seemed to be changing. They had nice horses for me to work with, and I was going to be showing again; and I never ate a dead hamburger again!

Cracks started showing up quickly, though. My boss would not hire qualified people to work around the horses or who were of any real help to me. I also noticed that his wife always wore very large sunglasses even when it was cloudy. The large glasses were not always successful in hiding the bruises, however. I eventually caught him in a lie, and when I confronted him on it, things went very bad very quickly. Not used to a woman who would stand up to him, he exploded into a rage almost instantaneously. Needless to say, I said, "I quit," at the same time he said, "You're fired."

I was a long way from Nebraska, so I called a girl I had met. She actually had worked on the farm with me, and we had become instant friends. But for some reason, my boss took a disliking to her and fired her, telling her she was never welcome on his farm again. I don't even know what set him off! She was a hard worker and excellent help for me. So I called her and asked if she might help me get my stuff off this farm. She said yes and got her parents to agree to let me put my things in one of their barns until my parents could come and help me get back to Nebraska.

She came over right away, and we were busy packing and loading our trucks. We were over in the barn getting my saddle and equipment I had brought with me when here he came, my boss, and he was livid. I have never seen such anger and rage in a human being as I did that night. His face was contorted, almost inhuman, and his eyes were burning with hatred and anger, and I didn't even know why. Mostly his rage was directed toward my friend; he was furious that she was back on his farm.

I tried to explain she was just there to help me leave, which was what he wanted, but there was no reasoning with him. I remember everything that happened next like it was yesterday. My friend was off about thirty-five feet to my left. My boss was to my right and in front of me about twenty feet. He was yelling at my friend, and she said something to him, and that was it for him. He now screamed at her, "I'm going to kill you!"

I had been looking toward my friend, but when I heard those words, my head jerked back to his direction, and without thinking, I said, "Kill her?" still not believing what I had just heard. I said, "You can't just kill someone." That's when his head turned toward me, and all of his attention was now focused completely on me! His face was bright red, his hands curled into two huge fists, eyes blazing with intense anger. His whole body shook with rage, and his eyes, crazy with anger, were now staring directly at me.

I probably should have been scared, but I wasn't. I had seen that anger before, stared into those eyes before, when I was six years old. It had scared me then, but not now I'm all grown-up and I wasn't intimidated. It didn't work with my dad, and it certainly wasn't going to work with this guy. It was then, with his gaze squarely on me, that he said these words: "I'm going to f——ing kill you!"

Without hesitating or thinking, I replied, "If you think you can, go for it." Of course, that was what I said. I had vowed to fight to the death years before, and that's exactly what I intended to do.

With hands still curled into fists, he ran at me. I stood my ground. He ran right up until we were nose to nose. And just like that night my dad had threatened to kill my horse, I believe this man saw the same thing in my eyes that my dad did—a darkness void of fear, void of emotion, void of anything except seething hatred. It was an anger just as intense as theirs and completely unwavering, and it caught them off guard. They were used to seeing fear and shock in other people's eyes. No, this was something new, something they had never seen before, and it scared them. We stood there, nose to nose, for a few intense seconds (seemed like hours), and then he told me, "You have one hour to get off my farm."

I replied, "I would have already been gone if you weren't out here bothering me."

With that, he stormed off, and we finished loading my stuff and left.

More Dead Ends

So that's how things went. I would go to work for someone I thought would be good, somewhere I could keep moving forward as a trainer, and just the opposite would happen. The next job I took was as an assistant trainer for a very well-known and successful trainer. In one summer, we hired forty-four different people, and forty-four different people quit. This guy treated people so bad they just quit, and I would be left to do everything—feeding, cleaning the stalls, grooming horses for the trainer—and I ended up giving lessons in the evenings because the wife decided it was too much work. I was hired to help work horses, period. Needless to say, after a year of this, I was exhausted and completely burned out.

It was on a very cold winter day, when the trainer was out of town, that I decided the two other girls working there and I needed a break. So we went in to the only warm place in the barn—the lounge area that was still under construction. There were a couple of guys in there hanging drywall. We came in, found some chairs, and sat off to the side so we weren't in the way. We talked quietly among ourselves, but it was a small room, and it wasn't long before the construction workers were sitting with us, laughing and talking. After some time, one of the guys looked right at me and said, "Wow, you're actually fun! We all thought you were not very friendly."

I looked at him and said, "Better a bitch than a whore." Absolute shock came across his face—his eyes got big, his smile quickly faded, and he was left speechless. I didn't care; I just kept talking. It had become quiet for a moment, and everyone was looking at me, not sure of what to say or how to react to such a statement, but I just continued on, and slowly everyone returned to the conversation.

The man I said it to, however, sat stunned at my words, and after several minutes of just sitting there, he looked at me and exclaimed, "Oh my god, you're right!" We all turned and looked at him, at which time he repeated, "You're right!" We sat, waiting for an explanation. He continued that the trainer (my boss) was always bragging about having sex with me and that every time I walked up to him and asked him something, when I walked away, he would make obscene gestures with his hips in my direction. Now it was my smile that faded, but my eyes didn't get big—they smoldered with anger and contempt.

This trainer was someone I had respected and looked up to since I was a little girl and whose ability to train I had marveled at, someone whom I worked my ass off for with never so much as a thankyou! Are you kidding me? Just as the construction workers perceived, I didn't talk to the construction guys, didn't look in their direction, and acted as if they weren't even there. I always knew exactly where they were, though. I was very aware of their presence, just never letting on that I was. I went out of my way not to flirt with anyone and not to give off any wrong signals. No, I made it VERY clear I was not someone who flirted or slept my way to the top. VERY CLEAR!

I hated whores! Male or female, I despised any and all who slept around, especially those who were married, and this trainer was married. I lived in his basement! Like, how was that going to work! His wife was always there!

Anger and hatred rose up in me, like a bomb ready to explode, and everyone in the room felt it. All eyes were big now, and they were looking at me. There it was again—being judged when they didn't even know me, believing lies about me without ever asking my side of things. I felt like a horse had just kicked me in my stomach. And then there was this horrible feeling of falling—falling and falling, lower and lower, darker and darker. Then *bam!* You hit the bottom of the pit, and there you are, flat on your back, looking up, trying to see the top, but it's too far away, and it's way too dark to see anything. Anything but your failures, disappointments, and yet another betrayal. As I lay there in the darkness, I wondered, *Why is this sur-*

prising to me? Everyone betrays me. They always have and they always will. Get over it and start climbing.

Back in the room now and realizing that everyone was staring at me, I acted like I don't care that much. I pretended that I don't hate people (men) that much, pretended that I'd never been molested or raped, pretended to be normal. *Don't let anyone know how much darker your world just got, how you're losing your grip down in that pit, or just how hard it is to get back up and start climbing. No, just smile.* Funny how a smile can make everything okay. So that's what I did—with a big smile, I said, "Well, that's it, I quit!" Everyone started laughing, a nervous laugh at first, but then I joined them, and now we were all laughing and smiling, everyone greatly relieved I didn't explode on them. They were laughing, but I was merely pretending. I did explode on the inside. I gave full vent to my anger and hatred.

When the other two girls working there saw how he treated me, they also quit. The construction worker who had told me what the trainer was saying helped me move my stuff, and he let me put it in his garage until once again I could find a place to go to. The girls and I stayed on, of course, taking care of the horses until the trainer returned. Then we all quit on the same day with no notice.

While working for this trainer, I had met a guy, who, at first, was just someone to get drunk with, but over time, I realized he was different. He just kept coming around, didn't expect anything from me, and never tried to kiss me or hold my hand. He was funny and very good-looking, and I found myself relaxing around him, almost enjoying myself, but I kept a watchful eye on him and never dropped my guard completely. I couldn't—I mean, right? It was just a matter of time before he turned on me too. Wasn't it?

After about six months of hanging out together, he asked me if he could kiss me good night, and something inside me said, "Go ahead, say yes. It's okay." So I did. Months passed, and we were spending a lot of time together. Once, when we were talking, something came up that we disagreed upon. Not wanting to get into a fight with the one person I really liked, I tried to just drop it. But he persisted, and then he started questioning me, "Why don't you have more opinions about things? Why won't you really talk to me?"

Oh boy, here we go. He wanted me to open up to him, and that's never going to happen. Never. I liked this guy, and right now, he liked me, but if he got to know the real me, it would ruin everything. I just kept evading things, and now he was somewhat mad, asking, 'Why won't you talk to me? Why don't you trust me?"

Ugh! "Look," I said, "I am not going to fight with you."

"Why not?" he demanded. We were both standing now.

"Because you don't want to see me angry." (He had no idea he was talking to a ticking time bomb.)

"Why?" he demanded again.

"Because you don't understand. When I get angry, I say things—awful, hurtful, terrible things. I had developed a talent at a very young age on how to hurt people. I watch people, study if you will, get to know them, and then use what I know will hurt them against them. But I hate myself when I do this. I say such horrible things and then I see such hurt in their eyes. I hate it because it's not really me. The real me would never hurt people on purpose, but just sometimes all the hurt that's been done to me just comes out no matter how much I regret it."

I was pleading with him now. "Please just let this go. Please don't push me." He had no idea of who I really am, what I'd been through, what I was capable of, and I was desperate to keep it that way. "Please just stop," I said, but he didn't. He wasn't going to let this go, and then he said *something*—I don't even remember what, but it was the *one thing* that snapped me.

I angrily blurted out something awful—again I don't even remember what, but what I do remember is the look that came across his face. He was speechless and shocked, and his eyes—oh my god, his eyes. Crushing hurt looked back at me. As we stood in silence, I hated myself. I had warned him, though; he should have listened. But it's too late now. I'd done it—hurt the one person I liked and who liked me.

The weight of his look was too much I had to look down. It was then that he spoke, and I do remember what he said next. With a soft and quiet voice, he said, "I don't know what has happened to you or who has hurt you so bad that you would say something like that to me, but I am going to stay and find out."

What? Unsure if I heard right, I looked back up at him. His eyes still looked hurt, but there was something else, something I had never seen before—love and forgiveness. And for the first time in eight years since the night I had cried myself to sleep when my mom would not talk to me about the abortion, I cried. He immediately came and pulled me close to his chest and held me. I cried and cried. After eight long years of holding everything in, of everything that happened—I cried.

He kept his word. He stayed, and over time, I shared bits and pieces of what I had been through, never really able to share the whole story and not just because I was scared he would leave but mostly because I couldn't. I couldn't say too many things out loud because then that meant they really happened. It made it real, and if something is real, then you have to deal with it. I simply could not accept it as real, could not process so many horrible things. Just couldn't or maybe just wouldn't.

I fell completely in love with this man—well, as much in love as someone like me is capable of. We moved into an apartment together, and I just knew we would marry one day. Things seemed to be looking up except that I wasn't working with horses and I was secretly miserable. A phone call would change that. A man who had Arabian horses and who had met me at the Morgan farm found me and wanted to hire me. At first, I said no. I did not want to train Arabians. I was a Morgan girl, but he persisted, and I finally relented, reasoning I would just do this for a while and then get back to Morgans.

Again, at first, everything seemed fine, but very quickly I realized this family had problems. Whenever the wife and the husband were in the same room, the temperature would drop about fifty degrees. They could barely be decent to each other. The fifteen-year-old daughter was struggling with the fact that her parents hated each other. I just tried to stay out of it and do my job. But one day, it came crashing into my lap, and I found myself right in the middle of it.

It was the end of a long day, and I was sitting on an upside-down bucket, rolling up a leg wrap. The daughter had rushed into the barn and was getting ready to do the evening chores. She was putting a bale of hay in the small feed wagon when the father came in, yelling at her. She ignored him and kept loading hay. This made him madder, and he grabbed her by the shoulder and spun her around so she was looking at him. He said something, she smarted back, and he punched her square in the face, knocking her back onto the hay. Then he turned and looked at me. I was staring directly at him when he yelled, "What are you looking at?"

"An asshole," I replied. Oh, that made him furious.

He came running at me. I stood up, still rolling the leg wrap. Again, I was face-to-face with a real creep, and again I was not backing down. Whatever this guy was going to do or say, I wouldn't know because I'm pretty sure when he looked into my eyes, he saw something unsettling. I don't care how bad you think you are. Nobody had anger inside them like me, and no one was looking to explode on someone like I was. Just one wrong move in my direction, and I would unleash a fury on you like you couldn't even imagine. For every wrong that had ever been done to me, for every time my parents didn't protect me, for every pet my dad killed, for every lie that was spoken against me, for every time I almost died, for every betrayal. No, when he looked into my eyes, he saw the same thing the other guy had, the same thing my dad did—deep, deep darkness, a hatred so complete it would pull you in and envelope you. Maybe that was what scared them. For a moment, they were sucked into my world—a world much darker than their own, darker than they could have ever imagined. This darkness was so complete it penetrated to the very core of their being, and though not one of them would ever admit it out loud, this darkness was scary and unnerving. No, everyone who ever peered into the darkness of my eyes walked away. I'm not saying I was stronger, badder, or even better at fighting than these guys. I'm not even saying I would have won. What I am saying is that I was fully committed to my promise—fight to the death. I wasn't scared of the fight (remember, I train 1,200-pound horses—much stronger, quicker, and deadlier than any human). I wasn't scared to die. I was, however, prepared to kill.

And oh, how I wanted someone. I just needed an excuse, just one little spark to ignite the furry that was always simmering just beneath the surface, to pour out punishment on anyone dumb enough to pick a fight with me. I desperately wanted to inflict as much pain on someone that I was able to, to vent all of my pent-up anger, hatred, and hurt on to anyone even if it meant dying. Actually, I would have welcomed death—welcomed an end to all this suffering, all these dark feelings and emotions. That was it, really. I had promised not to commit suicide, but nothing was said about protecting yourself, so if you were to find yourself in a struggle, fighting for your life, fight as hard as you can for as long as you can. Cause as much pain as you can, and well, if you die, it wasn't your fault. You were only defending yourself, but finally there would be an end to all this pain.

He left, and I tried to comfort the daughter. Then a few days later, I quit.

Once again, I found myself without a job and unsure of what to do. I did, however, have a job offer to train horses back in Nebraska. But that wasn't an option; I was unwilling to leave the love of my life, although after many tearful nights, my boyfriend could take it no longer. He told me, "I think you should take the job in Nebraska."

I was devastated. "How could you say this to me? I thought we were in love. I thought we were going to get married." There were several tense and many tearful days when he told me he would move with me. I was overjoyed. I took the job, made the arrangements, but as the day to leave approached, he wasn't packing anything.

He told me, "You move back and make sure you like it, and then I will come later."

I moved. He never did.

Meeting Jesus

Now I was back in Nebraska, back where everything had happened, back in the very town where the attack and rape had happened— back and utterly alone. I hadn't been worried; my boyfriend would be here soon—here to protect me, keep me safe. But he didn't come, and now fear crept in—unreasonable, penetrating fear. This was new for me. I had never really dealt with fear. It apparently had been buried far beneath the anger and seething hatred I had for pretty much all people. These were unexpected feelings, and they left me feeling vulnerable. I was after all back and in near proximity to those who had hurt me the worst.

I was confident that my molester would discover where I was and that I would more than likely run into my attacker at the grocery store, and it didn't take long for the fear to take control of me. I found myself unwilling and unable to do anything or go anywhere. I was terrified to leave my apartment to go to work, to go buy food, to do anything. Trapped in my own apartment, my boss soon wondered what had happened to me, and I eventually ran out of food. It was then that my mom called. My boss had called her to see if she had heard from me. By then, I was very sick. It had started as a cold, but with not eating much, it quickly developed into much more. I told my mom I was just sick and that's why I hadn't been at work. I don't think she believed me, but that was all she got out of me.

A short time later, there was a knock on my door. I peered through the peek hole to see my dad standing there. Great, not at all who I wanted to see, but I opened the door and returned to the living room floor and the blanket I had been lying on. He walked in, stood there a moment, and then grumbled, "Well, are you just going to lie there and be sick?"

"What do you want me to do?" I replied.

"Get up, and I will take you to the ER." At the emergency room, they discovered that I was very sick with walking pneumonia, so they gave me medicine and sent me home.

A few days later, Friday, my mom appeared at my door. It seemed our conversation had bothered her, and she came to see me in person. She lived about three hours away; she and my dad lived apart since the bank closing. Dad had moved to the same town I was in.

Shocked at my food situation, she immediately went to the store. Upon returning, she stocked my cupboards and made me some homemade soup. It was wonderful. Feeling some better from the medicine I was on, my mom and I started talking, and I'm not sure if it was my weakened state from being sick or if I just couldn't hold it in any longer, but I could see that my mom wasn't leaving until she understood why I would not go and buy food for myself. So I told her everything, from the time I was six years old until right then.

She just sat there, speechless, motionless, void of anything that I could see. I'm guessing she was numb. How does a mom feel when her twenty-six-year-old daughter tells her she was sexually abused for years, tortured and beat, raped not just once but twice and all under her watch? I never told her about the suicide attempt or the excessive drinking. That might've been too much.

After a few awkward moments of silence, she spoke. I was thinking, *Now I will get that hug, or at the very least, "I'm so sorry."* Uh, no. She said, "I think you need to talk to someone about this."

I thought to myself, *I am. I'm talking to the one person I've always wanted to talk to.* Standing, she went to a drawer, pulled out the phone book, and started looking for a psychiatrist. She called several numbers, and then after talking briefly to one of them, she said, "I found someone who seems very nice, and she will get you in right away today, so go get dressed."

I give up. She just isn't going to talk to me. Maybe this other lady will.

Maybe it wouldn't be so bad talking to a complete stranger. I mean, I could fool her just like I have everyone else, if need be. I have to admit, I was terrified to talk to this woman, but she was actually nice, and the best thing about her was that there was no condemnation in her eyes. I found myself sharing way more with her than I thought I would, even looking forward to meeting with her. She tried really hard to help me, and in some ways, I know she did, but eventually I quit going. I thought I had evolved enough. At least, I was able to return to work and go to the grocery store. Good, done with that! I was better now—or so I told myself. Just try not to think about the nightmares you're having, the one where you relive the attack over and over and over again—thrashing and struggling to breathe, unable to scream for help, waking up gasping for air, soaked in sweat, heart racing. They were the same every single night. I fought for my life every night. I felt the agony of suffocating every night. It was a constant onslaught on my mind, body, and soul, pushing me deeper into the darkness I had grown so accustomed to. Sliding ever downward, I realized what I thought had been the bottom of the pit was merely a ledge that had given way. It seemed there was no end to my misery, no real relief, and if that wasn't bad enough, with the darkness fully engulfing me, I noticed something about this pit. The air seemed to have changed somehow—it was heavier, harder to breathe.

Still reeling from the fact that my boyfriend had never moved back and, even worse, wanted to see other people, I was trying to move on. It was an impossible task, as every song on the radio reminded me of him. Every time I saw a car like his, I cried. It was horrible. Working horses was my only reprieve. Riding young and or naughty horses requires a great deal of concentration—if you don't want to get hurt, that is. I was starting a lot of new horses, and they did keep me focused on them and so kept the darkness at bay, even for just a few hours. Once again, horses were saving me.

Someone else who was helping me was my new farrier. He was the guy who took care of the horses' feet and put their shoes on, although I didn't see it as help at all. In fact, I didn't like him right off the bat. For some reason known only to him, he saw fit to share with me that he had had an affair on his wife but then found God, asked his wife to forgive him, and everything was hunky-dory now. Not exactly his words, but it was exactly what I was thinking. I took an immediate dislike to this guy and spent as little time around him as possible. Only problem was, it was required of me, part of my job, to take him to lunch, which I dreaded with every fiber of my being. I never talked much and was not even all that friendly toward him. Undaunted, he chattered away like an annoying bird. He was always talking about God. *Give me a break. You screw up, nearly lose your wife, and now you're going to use God as an excuse to make it okay? Whatever. You're a loser, and I don't like you and I don't want to hear anymore about how God found you and saved you and changed you. Once a loser, always a loser in my book. Don't care what your book says. Quit quoting scripture to me, I'm not buying it!*

Oh my gosh, this guy was as relentless as my nightmares. Please just shut up! So we were at lunch, and this time, he went too far. He told me the only way to get to heaven was by asking Jesus into your life—out loud—and asking Him to be your Savior. That was it for me.

Slamming my hamburger on to the plate, I pointed my finger at him and said, "Don't tell me my mom is not going to heaven."

I was staring at him with angry eyes, and apparently unbothered by this, he returned my gaze and said casually, "If she hasn't accepted Jesus, then yes, she's not going to heaven."

I was done with this guy. I threw some money on the table and went to the car, expecting him to follow, seeing as I was his only ride back to the barn and his truck. Nope, he sat in there, ate his whole lunch, and strolled on out and got in the car. Of course, I was even more mad because he sat in there and ate his lunch and I was still hungry.

The next time I had to take him to lunch, I changed my tactics. Instead of trying to ignore him, I slammed him with questions, one right after another. I knew I would trip him up, but dang, no matter what I threw at him, no matter how difficult the question, he answered me with scripture from the Bible. Not just sort of or once in a while, but every single question, every single time he could answer with Scripture and spot-on answer me. I didn't tell him, but that kind of freaked me out. I made him prove it, of course, so he kept his Bible close. I would ask, he would answer, and then he would open his Bible and show me. Well, I just needed to up my game a little, thinking of harder questions.

I never tripped him up, and after some time, my anger and annoyance turned to "How exactly does he do this?" As more time passed, I grew more and more fascinated with his ability to answer all of my questions like this. What used to make me mad now left me wondering if maybe I had been wrong about this guy, wondering what he knew that I didn't know. Maybe he wasn't such a loser after all. Now I couldn't wait to go to lunch and we started going to supper too, so we could have more time to talk. I would ask him questions late into the night, but now it was different; it was friendly. We laughed a lot, he explained a lot, and I thought a lot. He lived in Kansas and came to the barn about once, maybe twice, a month and would usually spend one night before heading back. I began to be sad when he left. I had grown very fond of our talks.

Every time he was about to go, he would look at me and say, "Remember, when things are hard and you're at your lowest, just reach out to Jesus. Just ask Him into your life, and He will come and He will transform you."

Eventually, there was a problem between him and my boss, and he quit coming. I felt very alone again. Our talks had become quite important to me; they were a bright spot in my very dark world. Again, I felt very betrayed. Just when there was something, someone, good in my life, it would be taken away by someone else. I slid a little further. On an extra dark day, I took his advice and asked Jesus into my life. I was in my car sitting at a stoplight. There were no trumpets blowing or bright lights flashing, but there was this incredible sense of a huge weight being lifted from me, like I could pick my shoulders up and breathe easier. It was a tremendous feeling, and from that day on, I never had that nightmare again—ever.

I started praying again. I had prayed long ago as a little girl, but somewhere along the way, I had quit, not consciously, of course. They were working too. It seemed like everything I asked for happened. Unfortunately, I never asked for the right thing, the one thing I desperately needed—healing.

No, I asked for things like help with a troublesome horse. It got better immediately—help in the show arena. I won. This was utterly amazing to me! My friend had been right—reach out to Jesus, and He will save you, help you.

It's just that I wasn't around my friend long enough to know the right things to ask for or what to do next. I mistakenly thought, *Okay, so now I have Jesus. Everything will be okay, and I'm better now!* Wow, was I wrong, and it was a very short time before I found out just how wrong I was!

You must remember, when you are a very broken person, you ask very broken questions. In fact, you don't even know enough to know to ask the right question. I saw life through a very dark and cracked glass, so everything I did, said, and thought came from a very skewed perspective.

The reality was that I didn't know I was broken. Hurt, betrayal, pain, darkness—it was all I knew, all I had ever known. How exactly would a broken person fix their broken life, anyway? How would that work? If you've only known betrayal from those who were supposed to protect you, how do you trust? If you've only known sorrow, what does joy look like? If you've only known darkness, what would light be like?

If you don't know what these things look like, how would you ever get to them? The answer is, you don't. You don't get to them—not by yourself, anyway. The help I needed was right there in my hand—within my reach—but I foolishly let it slip out and fall by the wayside. Once again, I had walked away from Jesus. With no guidance, I did what I had always done—stumbled on my own. Of course, I didn't ask for healing because I didn't know I needed it. I thought I had everything under control. Not talking about it equaled it not happening. Denial had become my best weapon for attempting to deal with all that had happened to me. Besides, I was not about to tell someone and then see sympathy in their eyes. I don't need or want your sympathy; I don't need anything from anyone.

Through all of this, I never felt sorry for myself. This was just life, after all. Bad things happened to everyone, it's just the way it is.

So I had stumbled my way back to Jesus and was praying but still found myself very alone—until I met someone. She was funny, she knew a bunch of people, and she liked me. So I started going out with her, and yes, it didn't take long before I was drinking heavily and closing down the bars with my newfound friends. Church, reading the Bible, Jesus—they all went by the wayside. Being drunk was truly the only way I knew how to drown out that voice inside my head and the darkness for just a little while. All I had ever wanted was to be able to dance like you were truly happy, laugh like you really meant it, take a deep breath and not have it burn all the way down, wake up glad to be alive. The darkness of the pit, my mind, my thoughts—they were crushing me. The blackness was winning. Every moment that I stayed alive, it was winning, and there seemed nothing and no one—not even Jesus—who could help me. So I drank.

Well, I may have walked away from Jesus, but He had not walked away from me, and He was nowhere near done with me. And on August 17, 1992, He yanked me back into His world. He was done with the drinking and denying, done with the self-destructive thoughts and behaviors, and He gave me an ultimatum.

Second Chance

I was on my way to pick up a horse some people had bought for their daughter. I was on a gravel road, in an old pickup truck with a two-horse bumper pull trailer. The truck was so old you couldn't run the air conditioner and pull a trailer at the same time. So it being August and very hot that day, I had both windows down. As I pulled on to the gravel road, I noticed a semi parked alongside the road about a quarter mile ahead. The driver, who was outside of the truck, turned and looked toward me and then climbed into his truck. Having a feeling that he was going to pull out in front of me, I slowed down some, and of course, he did. He must have really put the hammer down too—he tore off, causing a huge dust trail behind him.

If you've ever driven on dry, dusty gravel roads, you know what I'm talking about. For those of you who haven't, the dust trail a big truck leaves can envelope your vehicle and stretch out a mile behind them, depending on whether or not there's wind. There was not even a slight breeze that day, and the dust cloud seemed to remain indefinitely. I tried to avoid it by slowing more, but it completely covered my truck, and with the windows down, it filled the cab to where I was choking and coughing. It was awful! I pretty much just had to stop and wait for it to settle. I was unable to see anything.

At last, I was able to continue and I could see the end of his dust trail up ahead of me. I made sure to stay back and keep it in front of me. But as I came over a hill, I noticed it seemed closer. At the bottom of the hill was a T-intersection. You could only turn right off the road I was on, and the end of the dust cloud was about three quarters of the way through the intersection. I thought maybe it was lingering longer because it was at the bottom of a hill, and there were some trees off to the left, so it was kind of stuck there.

As I came down the hill, I continued to slow down. I did not want to choke on his dust again. I was getting closer and closer, and the dust was just staying there. I was slowing to somewhere between twenty and twenty-five miles per hour when all of a sudden, there was the end of his truck! *What is going on? He should be a mile away by now! Holy crap, it's coming right at me!* All I had time for was, "Oh sh—t!" and I slammed my right foot on the brake!

When I opened my eyes, I thought I was waking up from a dream, but then I saw my windshield all cracked and broken, the hood of my truck smashed up against the windshield, and then a feeling came over me—an understanding of what just happened. I knew right then in that moment what God was saying to me: "This is your last chance to change."

Without hesitating, without having to think it through, I said, "Please forgive me, God. I will change my ways." And then I said something that at the time I had no idea why I did. I said, "Please don't let me be paralyzed."

In those first moments, nothing hurt. I didn't even know I was hurt anywhere. Then I saw the driver leaning out of his truck, looking back at me, and I yelled to him for help. I couldn't move. The steering wheel was so close to my chest, and my legs wouldn't move. I was stuck, trapped, and feeling a little panicked. I wanted out!

At first, he wasn't going to come back and help. He thought I was bleeding. I assured him I was not, but I was afraid it might catch on fire and I needed his help to get out. So he finally came back and tried to open my door, but it wouldn't budge. He went to the passenger side, and it wouldn't budge either. So I held out my hand to him, and he pulled me toward him.

As soon as I got free of the steering wheel, I looked down, and the side of my right foot was on the side of my right knee! *Oh no!* I thought. *This is going to hurt.* So I said, "You know what, I think I'll just stay right here!" But he gave another hard jerk and pulled me to the passenger door, and yup, it hurt! He then grabbed me by my armpits and pulled me through the window, my very broken leg smashing into the door on the way through. He started to set me down, and I was, like, "My leg's broken. Maybe you shouldn't put me in the road," so he carried me to the ditch and lay me down. Again, I was watching my right leg as he set me down. When my foot touched the ground, my leg bent in half in the middle of my shin. Now he was asking me what to do, and I said, "Isn't there a farmhouse back up the road a bit?" He replied, "Yeah," so I said, "Can you go there and see if someone is there and call for help?"

He took off running with a bunch of keys hanging off his belt, and I could remember the sound of those keys shaking, getting farther and farther away until I couldn't hear them at all. I felt very alone at that moment, and then I realized I was having a hard time breathing, and wow, did my neck hurt! It was burning, painfully so, and I started to panic a little. It was swelling up, and I thought I was going to suffocate and die lying alone in this ditch. I had to lie there and talk to myself to keep my breathing slow and not panic, taking small, slow breaths so as not to hyperventilate.

Eventually, I heard a vehicle approaching. It was the driver of the truck and the farmer who lived in the house. He had called 911, and the ambulance was on the way. When they got there, I told them, "My leg is broken and my neck hurts, but please do not put my leg in an Aircast (because I knew how bad that would hurt). Just get me to the hospital where they have good drugs!"

The lady said, "Hey, Frank, get the Aircast." *Whoa, lady, what part of no Aircast did you not get?* So we started arguing about it. Of course, I lost, and it was agonizingly painful. They got a brace on my neck and strapped me down and off to the nearest hospital, which was a little rural one with one doctor on staff and a couple of nurses. So you have no idea how bumpy a gravel road is until you're lying on a board with a badly broken leg. It was nearly unbearable, but I was more concerned with my neck, and I didn't know why. I asked the people in the ambulance if they were praying people and if they would please pray that I would not be paralyzed. Again, I have no idea why I was asking this.

Once at the hospital, I thought they would give me some pain medicine, but I was completely wrong about that, and it quickly became clear to me that this doctor wanted me out of his hospital as soon as possible! He was grouchy and wouldn't answer any of my questions. I kept asking, "What's going on? What do the X-rays show?"

He was right behind me, talking with the nurses like I wasn't even there! It was so frustrating; they literally had my forehead and shoulders duct-taped to the board I was on. I couldn't move, couldn't see them. All I could do was stare at the ceiling. Finally, out of complete frustration, I yelled out, "What the hell is going on?" The very grouchy doctor leaned over my head so I could see him and blurted out, "Your neck is broken," and then went back to talk to the nurse!

"What? Wait a minute! What do you mean my neck is broken?" My mind couldn't really grasp that thought. All kinds of thoughts and feelings started flashing through my mind, and no one would talk to me! So I started moving my toes and fingers greatly, relieved that I could.

One of the nurses finally told me, "We are making arrangements to get you to a Lincoln hospital. Is there someone we can call, a family member, that could meet you there?"

I told them to call my mom, but I very emphatically told her NOT to tell my mom that my neck was broken! "Just tell her that my leg is broken because she has a two-and-a-half hour drive to get to Lincoln, and if she's too upset and freaking out about my neck, she might get into a crash and be hurt or killed." I warned her several times. "DO NOT MENTION MY NECK!" This was before cellphones, and the phone was on the wall not far from where I was lying, so I could hear her very clearly.

She started off, "Hello, is Mrs. Hesson there?" because my mom was at work at the time. "Hi, Mrs. Hesson, I'm Nurse so-and-so calling to let you know your daughter has been in an accident and has a broken neck." OMG, what? I started freaking out as the nurse continued, "Your daughter is being taken to Lincoln, and we thought you would want to be there."

She hung up, and now I was yelling, "You stupid idiot! I told you not to tell her about my neck. How are you that stupid?"

She tried to defend herself, playing it off as no big deal, which only infuriated me more. Now I was shaking and fighting against the restraints, trying to free myself, which got the other nurses concerned.

Fearing I would injure my neck further, they were pushing down on my shoulders, trying to calm me down, but I was not having it.

Realizing I couldn't break free, I screamed at her, "You are so lucky I can't get off this table because I would absolutely beat you to death!" Then I made a promise to her, saying, "You'd better hope and pray that nothing happens to my mom on her drive down because if anything does, once I'm able to get off this board, I WILL COME FIND YOU AND I WILL HURT YOU!"

While all this was going on, the doctor had spoken with the Lincoln hospital and found out there was no neurosurgeon on duty there that day, so they decided to have me taken to Omaha instead, where there was both an orthopedic surgeon and neurosurgeon working. By the time they figured this all out, they made the arrangements with the hospital and got life flight on its way to pick me up, fearing a long ride in an ambulance would jeopardize my neck. They realized that my mom was on her way to the wrong hospital, so they called the police who put them in contact with a sheriff on patrol on the very highway where my mom was driving on. They had me describe her car to them and asked him to watch for her. So now my mom, who was already in a state of panic driving to Lincoln, saw the flashing lights of a cop car. She pulled over, even more distraught now, thinking she had done something wrong.

When the sheriff walked up to her window and asked, "Are you Mrs. Hesson? Mother of Janel Hesson?" that was it for my mom. Fearing I had died from my neck injury, she started sobbing and screaming uncontrollably. The sheriff leaned in, putting his hand on her shoulder, desperate to calm her down. He said over and over, "She's okay, she's okay. Your daughter is okay. They're just taking her to Omaha instead of Lincoln, and I was just trying to catch you so you can go there instead." Finally, he reassured her that I was fine, and she regained her composure enough to thank him and resume driving. Only now she didn't know what to do. She sort of knew her way around in Lincoln but definitely not Omaha.

So unsure of what to do, she drove to my home in Lincoln and called a friend of mine, who dropped everything, left work, and drove my mom to the hospital in Omaha.

Once in Omaha, it was a long day of excruciating pain, as they would not give me any pain medicine until all of the doctors had looked at all of the X-rays. I didn't know it at the time, but they were actually discussing and trying to decide if they should amputate my right leg just below the knee or if they might be able to save it. All agreed to amputate, save one. A brilliant orthopedic surgeon said, "No, I can save her leg." The neurosurgeon studied my neck X-rays and decided the best treatment would be for me to wear a halo.

After measuring me, they realized they did not have one small enough for me and had to have one especially made. It would take three days for the halo to be delivered, so I spent three days being duct-taped to the board they brought me in on. That in itself was almost unbearable. Boards are very uncomfortable! But that was nothing compared to when they actually put the halo on! There was nothing like having to lie there while someone took a torque wrench and screw actual screws into your head!

Well, I did not just lie there. My arms were not taped down now, and I went for the doctor who was inserting the screws. There were four nurses trying to hold my arms, but they were not able, so eventually they turned to my brother, who was much stronger than them, to try. He was able, but it was devastating to him to be the one to hold my arms while I screamed in agonizing pain. When they were done, they gave me a huge dose of morphine, and I was finally able to fall asleep.

I guess I need to back up here and explain more of what my family went through once the word of my accident was out. My mom and friend arrived at the hospital shortly after I had. My mom spoke at length with the life flight nurse, who had taken care of me in the helicopter. She told my mom she had never met someone like me, explaining how the whole time in flight, even with a tube down my throat in case I became nauseous and had to throw up (the tube would keep me from suffocating on my own vomit), I had talked only of her and how worried I was if she would make the trip okay.

I don't remember what I talked about, only how nice this nurse was to me. The only thing I do remember telling her was that I had always wanted to ride in a helicopter! Just a tough way to do it, though!

My dad was working for a friend of his who had a trucking company. He did the bookkeeping and salaries, and if they were short a driver, he would drive for them too. This particular day, he was driving for them and was on his way to Kansas. Once again, no cell phones, so my mom had called his boss, who called ahead to the grain elevator in Kansas where he was delivering a load of soybeans, and told him when he got there what was going on. His boss' son was actually there, and since his truck was already unloaded, they switched trucks so my dad could turn around and come right home. It was a five-hour drive for him to get back to his pickup and then another hour to the hospital where I was at.

He got there about four in the afternoon, just at the same time some resident decided that he needed to scope my knee because it had a little cut on it, which, of course, I thought was completely unnecessary. I asked him if my knee was bleeding, and he said, "No," so I told him to put a Band-Aid on it and leave me alone. But he didn't, and it hurt a great deal. So I made sure he knew all about it and argued with him the whole time. He got done and walked out into the waiting area where my mom and friend were at and just as my dad was walking in.

Exacerbated, the resident looked around at my family and exclaimed, "Well, she's certainly feisty!" With great relief, my dad started laughing, deciding that if I was okay enough to argue with the doctor, I wasn't going to die!

My oldest brother, who lived in Iowa, arrived a little after my dad and was actually the first person they allowed in to see me. It was weird. I had been fine all day, just upset that the residents at this hospital took great joy in taking my Aircast off and on—which was incredibly painful—to show each new resident that came on staff how, if they pushed on the top part of my leg, it moved at the bottom. Each time I begged them not to do this, they didn't seem to care how excruciating this was to me! So finally, late in the day, in more physical pain than I had ever been in, I yelled at the top of my voice, "Stop pushing on my f—cking leg!"

One resident leaned over my face so I could see him and said, "You know there are children present." I don't normally swear in public, but I was at the end of my rope, and I blurted out, "How the f—— would I know? I'm taped to the g——damned board, staring at the g——damn ceiling!"

That was it for pushing on my leg. From then on, they left me alone.

Time on that day blurred together for me, but it seemed not too much after they let my oldest brother in. As soon as I saw him, the dam broke, and I started crying and telling him how much I loved him and how happy I was to see him. I thought I would never see any of my family again! I was much more scared of my broken neck than I cared to admit or even realized.

I have two other brothers, one who lived in Nebraska and one in Florida. The one from Nebraska made it after I was finally given pain medicine and was knocked out. The one from Florida who had taken the first flight he could got to the hospital by ten o'clock that night. He would stay by my bedside for well over a week. Unwilling to leave, the nurses finally gave up trying to make him leave when visiting hours were over. They eventually just brought him blankets and a pillow, and he slept in the chair next to my bed.

The first surgery on my leg would last eight hours. They inserted a rod and a titanium plate with nine screws holding it in place. I was in a full leg cast for several months and eventually one up to my knee. The leg was not healing, though, and after one year, they decided to do another surgery, where they would take bone from my hip and apply it to the large area where my leg was not healing. I would be on crutches for another full year before my leg was finally strong enough to put some weight on it. I had been on crutches for two years—two agonizing years full of discouragement, depression, and hopelessness. Unable to walk, unable to ride horses, I watched as everything I worked so hard for slipped through my fingers. I did eventually return to riding and the agonizing task of rebuilding my business—again.

I did, however, keep my promise to God. I quit drinking and partying and slowly but surely started climbing up out of the pit…again.

Climbing Again

I would like to say that after the accident and the two-year recovery, I got my life together and everything was great. But unfortunately, that's not how it went. It's true I wasn't drinking anymore, and I was back to going to church and reading my Bible, but I still was in a very dark place—still very broken, still trying to appear normal.

I limped along, putting everything I had into my business. I was able to buy a farm of my own with the money I got from my settlement of the accident. With quiet determination, I went about rebuilding myself and my business. And within a couple years, my barns were full of horses in training, and I had several employees. I thought that if I just had enough horses, won enough in the show arena, then I would be happy and would simply forget all I had been through. It sort of worked. I mean, it was like putting a Band-Aid on a huge gushing wound. But it temporarily slowed the gushing of blood that flowed through my brokenness, and I just became adept in my replacing of Band-Aids.

One Band-Aid that I tried only tore open the wound worse. I had decided to marry someone I knew I shouldn't!

I chose to ignore ALL of the red flags and married him, anyway. Ugh, another horrible decision that I would live to regret! I actually was going to call it off the night before we got married, but not wanting to disappoint my mother, I went through with it and immediately started paying for it on our wedding night at the reception. I won't go into details, but I will tell you that after having shared with him about being raped, he did something completely demoralizing, degrading, and with absolutely zero thought of how I would react or feel. I felt victimized once again, only this time by someone I thought I could trust. In actuality, I should have known better; there were red flags and signs that should have alerted me to impending danger. But I was so completely broken on the inside my internal compass didn't work at all. I had never had a healthy relationship with a human ever! I never learned what true love looked like or what a trustworthy person would be like, and what he did caught me completely off guard. I was instantly horrified, and my head started spinning, I felt nauseous as if I was sucker-punched in the gut. And on my wedding night, I found myself falling again—falling back into the abyss of darkness that I had been fighting so hard to leave. His friends were laughing and cheering and clapping their hands—while I was falling.

I turned and looked at the girl who had helped me with planning the wedding, and she pointed at me and said, "We got ya!" *Boom!* I hit the bottom. Once again, the people I thought were on my side, thought I could trust, turned on me. I was publicly humiliated, and maybe my friend didn't know everything I had gone through, but he did. He knew because I told him, and without a single thought of what it would mean to me, with absolutely no regard to the precious information I had shared with him, he treated me like nothing more than a common whore, a conquest—just like so many before him.

Instead of joy and happiness on my wedding night, I found myself back in that house, full of darkness and fear. Emotions and feelings that I worked so hard to bury came rushing back, flooding my mind and body—the feeling of being absolutely powerless to help myself, of being insignificant and unloved. The rest of the night was a blur, my head reeling from the flood of old emotions that came immediately back to the top of my consciousness. My heart was broken again by the complete lack of regard by someone I had finally confided in and trusted to actually care about me and my feelings. It only confirmed what I already knew: No one could be trusted. No one gives a damn about you. You are simply something to be used by them for their own sick pleasure. It completely confirmed that I was worthless and unlovable.

The honeymoon in Hawaii that was supposed to be wonderful and amazing was a nightmare. We fought every single night we were there. We came home, and the fighting continued. I spent my days working my butt off—feeding, cleaning stalls, and training horses seven days a week. On the weekends, I was up at six feeding horses, working hard all day, training and giving lessons. By 5:00 p.m., I would be done with the lessons, would feed the horses, and would be back in the house by 6:00 p.m. His Saturday consisted of sleeping till noon, washing his pickup, lying on the couch, drinking Pepsi, and then yelling at me when I came in from work because supper wasn't ready, and I didn't feel like going out and dancing all night. I knew full well that I shouldn't have married him, but I found out much too late how completely different he was after being married. The fighting never stopped—sleeplessness began to take its toll on me, and it wasn't long before I found myself in the middle of depression. I was feeling trapped, as Christians aren't supposed to get divorced, and being new to this Christian lifestyle, I felt if I divorced him, it would put me on God's radar in a bad way. And not wanting God to be mad at me, I stayed in the marriage. Feeling like I was stuck forever in this horrible situation, I found myself lying at the very bottom of the pit I had fought all my life to get out of.

But now in the middle of a full-blown depression, every movement was excruciating. My muscles burned with pain all the time and just going to the bathroom had turned into a major ordeal! I would have to roll out of bed and fall hard to the floor. This effort left me exhausted, and I would just have to lie there until I could summon some strength to start crawling on my hands and knees. Too weak to stand, I would crawl a few inches and then collapse back to the floor, exhausted and sweating profusely like I had just run in the longest marathon ever. I would lie there a while and then summon a little more strength and then crawl a few more inches. It would take me several minutes to cross the ten feet to go to the bathroom, and upon reaching the toilet, I would lie on the floor until I could get up enough strength to get up and sit on the toilet. When finished, I would literally fall to the floor and start my crawl back to my bed.

The one good thing I had was a girl working for me who was great with the horses, and she helped me keep things going. After a couple of weeks in bed, I knew I had to get back to work. I really struggled, though. It was exhausting just getting up and getting dressed, but when working horses, I somehow found the strength. I'm pretty sure God gave me the strength to work horses because somehow, I managed to work all twenty every day. But at the end of the day, there was nothing left, and I would immediately go in the house, put on some pajamas, and collapse into bed. I rarely ate supper and would wake up the next morning to start the whole process over.

There was something about the horses, even though my beloved Agi Pat had died at the age of twenty-eight, one year after I had purchased my farm, and is buried on the farm. Something about them got me to get up out of my bed, out of my head, and to completely focus on them. Right in the middle of debilitating depression, they were still like a drug I needed. Yes, I had gone to several different doctors, different counselors, tried every kind of medicine they prescribed, and yet nothing worked—nothing helped except the horses. For eight to nine hours a day, my mind was free from the constant onslaught from the voice in my head, telling me, "You're worthless. You are nothing. No one cares. You should just kill yourself." These dark thoughts were all I heard—all I felt—every single minute of every single day, and the only way to fight them off was to focus on training the horses or by sleeping. So that was what I did—work horses, go to sleep, work horses, go to sleep. This was what I did, how I lived—if you call that living—for several years.

I poured myself wholly into my business and career, trying very hard to hide all the hurt, brokenness, and tribulation that went on in my mind all the time. I was up to thirty-eight horses in training and several employees, going to shows all over the country and having some success in the show ring. But no matter how hard I worked or how much I won, I could never seem to attain that feeling of happiness or contentment. So I worked harder, pushed myself more and more until I pushed myself right into mono. It was as devastating and just as bad as the depression, causing debilitating fatigue and horrific muscle pain; every fiber of my body hurt, and I developed crippling headaches. I was forced to take some time off, and then I went right back at it.

I figured that if I worked hard, everything would fall into place and I'd be successful. Going to church and reading my Bible would make me happy. I mean, everyone else at church seemed happy. I had started going to a new church. It was very different from what I was used to—people clapped their hands and raised them in the air when they were singing, they talked back to the pastor, and everyone was always smiling and friendly to me, going out of their way to shake my hand and greet me!

I remember the first time I went, and we were singing songs off a big screen at the front and not from a hymnal. There were drums and guitars like a concert! And I stood there, looking around. Everyone was so engaged in the singing, hands in the air as they were swaying with the music, and I thought to myself, *They all look so peaceful and happy. What is it they know that I don't? What was it about this church that made people so happy?* Well, I had no idea, but I knew one thing: I intended to find out.

The first five Sundays that I went, when the pastor started talking, I cried. I didn't know why or what was going on, but I couldn't help it or stop it. The tears just started flowing. At first, I was a little embarrassed. I tried hard to fight it and stop it, but every time I left that place, I felt a little bit better. I don't even know how or why I felt the way I did; I just know something inside felt different. So I quit fighting it all together. My then husband was coming with me to church, and he was highly embarrassed with me and the crying. It wasn't like I was loud or anything; I just had tears streaming down my face. There was no noise, but he hated it and would get really mad at me, telling me to stop and then yelling at me in the car on the way home. I didn't care. He could yell all he wanted. I knew something about me was changing; I didn't really know what was changing or why, but I was feeling different on the inside, and for whatever reason, I liked how I felt!

The marriage had gone from bad to worse. The fighting never stopped, and the tension and stress were taking a huge toll on me.

One time, I went to get my hair trimmed, and when my stylist started brushing my hair, she stopped and said, "Oh no!" Looking at me in the mirror, she held up her hand, which had a huge clump of my hair in it. Her eyes were big with shock.

I just stared at it, and then she looked a little closer and realized the ends had bulbs on them, meaning it wasn't breaking off but was coming out by the roots! By the handful!

She stopped brushing it and told me that she wouldn't be able to do anything with my hair, that this was really bad, and that I should go to my doctor immediately, which I did. He asked me if I was under a lot of stress, and I told him that I was. He told me I had to figure out how to change my situation or all of my hair would fall out, and then he gave me some medicine to take to try and help with the stress.

There were so many things going wrong in my marriage that I finally asked him to move out. I told him that I needed some time to figure some stuff out. We were separated for a year, then he moved back in, which was when he finally came clean about the affair he was having. Of course, I was upset but not all that surprised. And at first, what seemed like the worst thing ever became my way out. I finally had a legitimate reason to divorce him, and citing irreconcilable differences, we were divorced.

Going through a divorce is a very hard thing. Even though the marriage was never great, it was the death of a dream—the happy ever after and the white picket fence. It was just one more blow that pushed me further into the darkness. I felt like I was back at the bottom of the pit and had to start climbing again, which was a daunting task. I thought about just giving up. I mean, I was just so tired of climbing, who cared, anyway? Maybe I'd just lie here in the dark with the flames of hell licking at the bottom of my pit.

I kept going to that church, and with each week I went, I seemed to find a little strength, so I climbed a little. I found a little faith, so I climbed a little more. I felt like I was making some progress; I was definitely a long way from the top, but I wasn't on the bottom either. Things continued like this, and while I was trying to escape the pit and the darkness and the hopelessness that infiltrated every fiber of my being and every aspect of my life, I was still running my business, still traveling and showing, still trying to attain the success that I longed for. On the outside, things looked pretty good—my barns were full of training horses, I had several employees, and I was doing well at the shows I went to. But on the inside, I was fighting a losing battle. I still struggled with depression, my thoughts were oppressive, and there was a constant narrative in my mind. "You're not good enough, and no matter how hard you work, you're not enough. You will never be anything. No one cares about you. You don't even like yourself, why would anyone else like you?" Self-hatred grew until it consumed me, and the depression made just breathing hard. It felt as though an elephant was sitting on my chest and I was suffocating. Just being alive became an unbearable task. Every movement, every breath was a struggle.

Ultimate Betrayal

Yes, being at that church seemed to be helping. Everyone that went there seemed happy, and so I thought, *Now that I go here, so I must be happy too. Oh, good, I'm finally better!* I was a quick learner, and I figured out just when to raise my hands during the songs, the proper response when the pastor would say a certain statement. Yes, I had figured out how to fit right in! I had everyone convinced I was happy, even sort of had myself convinced I was happy right up until I heard this.

One Sunday, as he was preaching, the minister had made a statement. He said, "God loves you so much! He's just always taking care of you, always protecting you—"

What? Wait a minute, what was that last thing you said? God loves you so much that He always protects you? It was like a needle being dragged across a record that's being played. My mind started racing. *Protects? Protects? He protects people He loves? Uh, where exactly was He when I was six? Or how about when I was fifteen or when I was being raped?*

My head was spinning as thoughts poured in faster than I could process them! My whole life was flashing before my eyes—every agonizing moment in that house, every brutal attack! And then the worst thought of all: *God must not love me! If God protects the people He loves, then He couldn't possibly love me, or He wouldn't have let all these things happen to me!* And now a rage started to build in me. How could a six-year-old little girl do something so bad that God would not love her, would not protect her! How could an Almighty God turn His back on a little girl and let those horrific things happen to her! *Are you kidding me? Where were you, God?* I repeated the question over in my head, demanding an answer, and when no answer was given, my rage grew.

I never heard another word of the pastor or of the sermon. I just sat there, smoldering over what he said, over that fact that God would allow this stuff to happen to me, that He would love all these other people and not me. Talk about a sucker punch, and oh, did I hit the bottom of the pit hard! Maybe harder than at any other time. And I wasn't lying there, feeling sorry for myself. I was lying there, hating God for what He had done to me, for purposely not protecting me. Just when I thought things were getting better, just when I was making some headway in climbing out of that damn pit, the biggest sucker punch of all, the biggest betrayal of all, the darkest thought of all—*I'm so bad not even God loves me.*

I just lay there, my mind trying to reason things out, and really all I could think about was, what could a six-year-old child do that would cause God, Creator of everything, to turn His back on her? To cause Him to not love her and protect her? Why would He allow all these horrible things to happen to her? My mind really just got stuck there on that one thought. I spent hours, days racking my brain, trying desperately to remember something I did as a little girl to cause God to hate me so.

I continued going to church, thinking maybe I would get an answer to my question. But I never did, and the more I heard the pastor talk about an all-knowing, omniscient, loving Father God, the more anger built up inside me. Loving Father, huh. The term repulsed me.

I was constantly struggling with my own thoughts. What had I done so long ago as a little girl that had angered God so? Was it the same thing that had angered my own dad so much? Was there something so inherently bad about me that everyone hated me, and was that why no one seemed to love me? God, what was it that I had done? My thoughts became even heavier and more oppressive, and I completely quit trying to climb out of my pit of depression and hopelessness. *Nope, not anymore. I'm too tired. I don't care anymore. It's hopeless.* I've tried my whole life to climb up and out of this pit, this darkness, this oppression, and it never works. I NEVER get out! So forget it. I'm going to lay right here and die in this damn deep black hole. The darkness had won, and I was completely swallowed up by it—completely engulfed in anger and hatred, contemplating suicide once again. My beloved horse had died, so I was released from my vow to stay alive and protect her. Life sucks, and it had definitely sucked all of my hopes, my dreams, my desires right out of me, leaving me lying alone at the bottom of a hole so deep; I was definitely a lot closer to hell than to heaven.

I had worked so hard my whole life to get up out of this pit—clawing and climbing, poring myself into my business, working twelve- to fourteen-hour days year after year. I worked myself into mono three different times. I was desperate to get out of the darkness and into that place of light and joy where everyone else lived, where everyone else's dreams were coming true. Successful businesses. Marrying and having kids. Everyone around me was moving forward, enjoying life, while I was stuck in a hopelessly deep hole. And no matter how hard I tried, no matter how hard I worked, no matter how hard I tried to be happy, I failed. I failed at every level. My business wasn't where I wanted it. My marriage was a colossal failure, and there was absolutely no joy anywhere in or near me. So why bother anymore? That's it, I quit! It simply hurt too much to have dreams and realize they are never going to come true, to work so hard only to see yourself getting older instead of closer to success or to joy or any kind of happiness. What happened to the little girl who had started out with so much promise, with big dreams and desires? Why had life come at her so hard and viciously when so young and still innocent?

I tried to reason all these things out in my mind, trying desperately to wrap itself around all this. But the more I tried to make sense of it, all the more my mind slowly started shutting down and with it my dreams, my hopes, and my desires shut down also. And I was back to being just a dark void, empty except for anger. Anger was all that I had left, and I gave full vent to it. After years of denial, years of pretending to be fine, I turned all of my attention to God, and on a Thursday night, I decided to have it out with Him. I was lying in bed—not sleeping, of course—seething with an intense hatred. The only conclusion my mind could come to was that God was a creep who took pleasure in my suffering, who helped other people but, for whatever reason, didn't see fit to help me. The conversation went something like this: "Loving Father, my butt. There's nothing loving about you! You're a cold-hearted bastard just like my dad! Cruel to people for no reason, just waiting for me to make a mistake so you can crush me. You can't do anything right! Look at your world and how screwed up it is and look at your people! A bunch of murderers, pedophiles, and rapists—you SUCK AT BEING GOD! I hate you, I hate this world, I HATE my life! And the only reason I don't kill myself right now is because it would just give you one more reason to be pissed off at me and send me to hell. So how about you just let me die in my sleep? You can stick me in the back forty of heaven, raking leaves—I don't care! ANYTHING would be better than this world!"

After venting on God, I eventually fell asleep, and when I woke up alive, I hated Him even more!

A Lifeline

It's Friday now and the day after telling God how much I hated him. It's also the day before I leave for my National's Horse Show with seven horses. Normally on that day, I would never leave my farm for any reason. I would get up, work the horses in the morning, and then load the trailer for the two-week trip in the afternoon. And so I was up, getting ready for work when the phone rang. I picked it up, and it was the wisest woman I had ever met. She was the leader of a Bible study group of women that I had gone to a few times. I didn't really like the group. I was very uncomfortable around groups of people, but I did like her. She was older and she possessed something I wanted—joy and peace. It just exuded from her, and I was drawn to her like a moth to the flame. She called to tell me about a young pastor from Zambia, Africa, whom she had met. She told me how impressed with him she was and that he was coming to a ladies' house here in town to speak and that she thought I should come and listen to him. I was polite because like I said, I really liked and respected this woman and told her I would try to be there. I hung up the phone with no intentions of going. I had to get ready for my horse show.

I went back to getting ready when another woman called me— the only other person I actually liked and respected. I had actually had met this woman at the church I was going to. We were both in a class the church offered to new people to figure out where we fit in and to learn about the church and the different programs it offered. I heard her talking to someone and I asked if she was divorced, and she said yes. And then we figured out we both have horses; it would turn out to be the beginning of a beautiful friendship. Of course, at the time, I only let her in a little bit to my world, thinking anyone who loved horses couldn't be all bad.

She told me the same thing, there was this young pastor who was amazing, and she thought I should go listen to him. Now I'm not sure why, and even though I hated God, two people that I really respect had just told me the same thing. Something inside me felt like I should go. And I'm not really sure why, but maybe out of respect to these two women, I agreed to go. It was the first time ever I changed the routine on the day before leaving for this big show. I called the guys who were working for me and told them there was a change of plans, that they could start loading the trailer, and when I got back, we would work the horses. So I went to my friend's house—the second woman who had called—and we rode together to see this guy.

On the way to the house where this guy was speaking, I shared with my friend exactly what I had told God the night before, and that when I woke up alive this morning, I hated Him even more. I think she was a little shocked at what I had said about God, but her eyes were full of compassion as she said, "I'm sorry you feel that way. Maybe this guy can help."

I nodded in agreement, thinking to myself, *No one can help.*

When we got to the house, we were a little late, and he had already started speaking. There must have been close to twenty people crowded into the small living room, so we sat on some chairs in the dining room that overlooked the living room. We were right behind the couch where several people were sitting but in direct view of this young pastor. What I tell you next is not an exaggeration at all and is the absolute truth.

As we sat down, he was telling everyone that even though he was young, he had seen a lot, been through a lot. He was "saved" (a term Christians use when they've accepted Jesus as their Savior) at gunpoint and knew of people who "hate God so much that they beg Him to let them die in their sleep, and when they wake up alive, they hate Him even more!" *Are you kidding me? Who is this guy, anyway?*

Trying to appear as though he wasn't talking about me, I just sat there, no change in expression, no outward sign to indicate anything was wrong. My friend's reaction, however, was quite dramatic and very obvious. Her head jerked toward me, mouth open in surprise, eyes big with shock. I thought to myself, *Oh God, stop looking at me!*

I stared straight ahead at the guy like I didn't know and didn't see the absolute shock on her face. Well, this guy definitely had gotten my attention, but when he actually went into his teaching or sermon or whatever you want to call it, he had much more than that. His words were like nothing I had ever heard before, like my ears could not believe what they were hearing. They were soft and sweet, and they lofted into my head like a gentle, beautiful melody. And somehow, they seemed to penetrate my very soul. I don't know how, but they broke through the cold hard wall I had put up as my defense. The ice inside me seemed to melt just a little. I felt vulnerable and unprotected. And yet there was no fear, no panic at being defenseless. No, quite the opposite, and for the first time in maybe ever, my spirit seemed to come to life, like I had waited all of these years to hear such words. It was warm and comforting—a completely new sensation for me! I didn't know what was happening to me and I definitely couldn't explain it. All I knew was that I wanted more, and even as broken as I was—even as much as I hated God—somewhere deep inside of me, I realized that I had found exactly what I had been looking for my entire life! And I was smart enough to know that this guy was the answer I so desperately needed. And in my head, I told God, "If you would let me quit my job right now, I would just follow this guy around like the disciples had done with Jesus."

When he was done with his teaching, he said, "Now I want to prophesy over each of you," although I had no idea what that meant. Then he said, "I don't really consider myself a prophet. I just overhear conversations in heaven about you."

Oh crap! Yep, I'm out. There is no way I want to hear what heaven is saying about me right now 'cause I know what I had just said to God all last night. So I decided I would just quietly leave. I needed to get back to work, anyway. That's when he asked, "Does anyone need to leave right away?" and of course, my friend shouted, "She does!" as she pointed at me. Ugh!

The pastor was looking right at me now and said, "Okay, I will do this woman here in the front and then you." When it was my turn, I had to go out into the middle of that living room in front of all those people. I only knew the two women who had called me. I was standing in front of this guy, very uncomfortable with being in front of so many people and not knowing what to expect. He looked at me and asked me my name and what I did for a living. And then he asked if he could pray in the Spirit for me.

I answered yes. I had no idea what he was talking about.

So he started praying and walking around me. I didn't understand anything he was saying, and then he stopped in front of me, his piercing brown eyes staring directly into mine, and began to speak. The first thing he said was, "People have been walking out on you your whole life."

This caught me off guard. How did he know this? He went on to tell me how bad things have been for me without ever saying anything anyone in the room would understand but me. My head was spinning. I didn't understand how this complete stranger could know so much about me. He said things that went straight to my heart. A tear trickled down my cheek, then another. Then he looked intently at me and said, "You're a joyful person, but you've never experienced true joy." Now tears were streaming down my face. He went on to tell me, "God doesn't hate you. He actually loves you, and you are going to do great things for God!"

My whole body was spinning now. Emotions were flooding through me that I'd never felt before. He told me I had an Esther anointing. Esther is a girl in the Bible who found favor with the king. My mind was whirling, trying to listen to what he is saying while at the same time trying to grasp what he was saying. The dam broke, and I was full-blown crying in a room full of strangers and I didn't even care. This complete stranger was telling me things about me he couldn't possibly know. Because NO ONE knew except me. NO ONE EXCEPT ME! Well, and maybe God. Yes, only God could know these things. I hadn't told any human anything. And so if this guy was telling me things because God had told him, then he must be speaking the truth. And if he's speaking the truth, then maybe, just maybe, God did care about me. I was still not completely sure that He loves me, but maybe—oh, just maybe—in all of God's infinite mercy and forgiveness, He just threw me a lifeline—a line long enough to reach all the WAY DOWN to the bottom of the deep dark pit I was lying in.

I left that meeting feeling different. I can't really say better but definitely different. My mind was whirling, and I almost allowed myself to have just a little bit of hope—hope that maybe God didn't hate me and maybe there was a way out of this pit, out of the darkness that pervaded all of my thoughts, all of my emotions, and every single heartbeat.

I went to my horse show, expecting things to be better. I mean, God had said some really awesome things about me. Maybe this was my new beginning. Maybe now things would work out for good and not bad. Maybe now my plans would succeed instead of fail miserably.

Wow, was I wrong. I had the worst show ever; my brother and I got into a huge fight, and I went out and got completely drunk. Yup, I failed at every level again. I knew better, though. I knew I should not get my hopes up—nothing ever works out. And now not only did I feel horrible, but I felt stupid, too—stupid for daring to get my hopes up even a little that things would be good or get better in any way. *I'm an idiot. Why would I listen to that guy, anyway? I'm never going to do anything great. I'm never even going to get out of this damn pit! This just hurts too much, and I can promise you I won't let it happen again. It will be a cold day in hell before I get my hopes up about anything.*

When I got home from the show, I told my friend who had gone to see the young pastor about how bad things had gone, and she told me several women were so impressed with this guy and that they were going to where he lived—about forty miles away—to Bible study with him at the church he helped at. She thought I should go with them. In all honesty, I didn't really want to, but even as crappy as things had gone, I could not shake that feeling of when he had started preaching. Somewhere deep inside of me, I longed to hear more of the same, and I still had this feeling that this guy had the answers I needed, so I agreed to go.

On the drive to go see him, I got to know the other women a little, and they all seemed really nice and were searching for answers as I was. They all wanted to know how things had gone for me at the horse show, and I told them how bad it had been. One of them suggested asking the pastor if I should quit training horses, that maybe God was trying to move me out of that profession. In my heart, I didn't feel like I should quit. I mean, horses were what had been keeping me alive all these years, but I certainly wasn't going to share any of that with these women I didn't know all that well. But maybe she was right. I had just had the worst show of my entire life. Maybe I should ask Him. I agreed and said I would.

Once again, as soon as this guy started speaking, things way down deep in me started to stir, and by the time he was done, I was really glad I had come along. That was about to change, though. After his teaching, he told us to move around or go sit wherever we wanted. He was going to turn on some worship music so we could all pray for about fifteen to twenty minutes. Then we would all gather at the front of the church to see if anyone had any prayer requests or if he had heard anything from God that he would share with us.

After about twenty minutes, he turned the music off, and we all stood at the front in a semicircle around him. He asked if anyone needed prayer or anything, and a couple people said yes, so he prayed for them, and then he said he had a word from God for a couple people. So he was doing his thing, speaking kind words of encouragement to one person and then healing to another, and then he turned and looked at me. His eyes did not look kind or encouraging. They seemed mad, and I thought, *Uh-oh, what now?*

He started by saying, "God is done with you not trusting Him! He's done, he said empathically!" He started saying, "God gave you a chance, and you blew it! And then he gave you a second chance, and you blew that too! And now He says it's time! It's time for you to trust Him!"

Now the pastor was pointing his finger at me and speaking harshly and angrily. Normally anyone who would have put their finger in my face would have lost that finger, but everything this guy was saying was the truth! I mean, he was right about EVERYTHING! I stood there and took it, secretly wanting to cry and run out of the building. But I stood my ground, publicly chastised by God in front of all those people.

The last thing he said to me was, "You are going to learn to trust God."

With that, he was done, and I could not get my coat on and out of that church fast enough. Just as we were going out the door, one of the ladies turned to me and said, "We forgot to ask him if you're supposed to quit training horses."

I looked at her and said, "That guy just yelled at me, and I am not about to go back in there and ask him anything!"

She said, "I will ask him for you. You just have to stand there."

I reluctantly agreed, and we made our way back in, everyone following, anxious to hear what he would say. So we walked up to him, and my friend briefly explained about how things weren't going well for me with my job and wondered if I should quit training horses.

He looked up toward the ceiling for a minute or so and then looked down at me and said, "Don't quit training horses because how you train horses is how you will train people one day."

Okay, I thought to myself, *what does that mean?* Too scared to ask him, I just nodded and headed for the door. Relieved about not having to quit training, I, however, left that place perplexed about what he had said—the part about training people.

I thought a lot about what he said. I found myself wanting to get my hopes up again, that maybe I would get up and out of this pit. But I quickly reminded myself of how agonizing and painful it was to get them up only to have them crushed before you. So I pushed all hope aside and resigned to just lie in the darkness. *I'm done with trying, done with climbing, done with having ANY kind of hope that I will ever be free from the darkness.*

In my mind and heart, I had given up, but whatever had happened to my spirit the first time I heard that pastor speak, whatever had sprung to life way down deep inside of me, had definitely not given up. And as much as I wanted to just lie there and die, it wouldn't let me. Every week, no matter how tired or how bad I might feel, something made me go to those meetings. And every single week when he was teaching, I was glad I was there. I hung on every word that came out of his mouth, sometimes learning more from when he was just talking about himself and his life than when he was teaching.

Like, one night, he was sharing with us how he had gone to his favorite Mexican restaurant and gotten takeout and rented a movie, excited to get home to eat his meal and watch the movie. He put the movie in, sat down, and just as he was about to take his first bite, he heard God say, "Go to the church and pray." Hoping he had heard wrong, he picked up his fork but he heard again: "Go to the church and pray." So he got up, turned off the movie, put his meal in the fridge, and went to the church to pray. He said, "I got there about 8:00 p.m. and left at midnight."

What? Are you kidding me? Who prays for four hours? I'm lucky to get five minutes in!

Then he went home, heated up his food, and watched his movie. Things like that just blew my mind. I mean, it was obvious that this guy really loved God. It was also obvious how happy he was, and not because everything always went right but because he genuinely loved God. I didn't genuinely love anyone, and it brought him great joy. I wanted to be happy like this guy, and God knows I needed some joy in my life. Listening to him, watching him interact with people, I found myself drawn to him. I couldn't tell you exactly why if you had asked me, but I never missed one of those meetings. His knowledge of the Bible and the wisdom with which he spoke was mesmerizing to me, and I couldn't get enough of it.

I had been going a few weeks now, and I began to realize things about me—things like how different I was from the other people there. Like how they would all talk and share things about their life and then they would pray for one another. I didn't share anything, and I certainly did not pray for people. I mostly kept to myself, rarely spoke, but I did listen to the pastor, listen to other people, and I thought a lot. I thought, *How could they trust enough to share such personal things? Why do they seem so happy? How does this young pastor know so much about God? How did he learn all this? Why does God talk to him like that? Why doesn't He talk to me? Why does God talk to these other people? What exactly do they know that I don't?*

I kept thinking and thinking about all these things when one night after the teaching, while the music was on and everyone was praying, a realization came crashing down on me. And quite suddenly, it dawned on me of just how broken I was. *I'm not like all these other people because I am utterly and completely broken. I have no joy in my life, no peace, no contentment because I have no idea what these things look like! I simply do not know—or maybe I should say, remember—what it is like to be happy. I mean, it seems like such a simple thing, but it completely eludes me. And why would I trust anyone enough to share things when every time I trusted someone, it caused great bodily harm to me? And love people? Love God? Are you kidding me? I don't even love myself, how would I ever be capable of loving someone else?*

All these thoughts came one right after another, and things that probably should have been obvious to me poured through my mind. It was like a dam broke, and one realization after another gushed out and into my consciousness—so much so that my mind felt like it was swimming, spinning, and churning. As one thought led to another and another, slowly a single thought worked its way to the top: *I am completely and totally messed up! Broken beyond repair!* It was wave after wave of realizations crashing down on me, and I was drowning. I was sitting right there in that church, with all those people praying and worshipping God, and no one even knew, even noticed, even cared. I felt as if I was in a mental battle for my life, surrounded by people and yet completely unable to yell out for help, for someone to throw me a life jacket.

And then a very familiar feeling came over me—a feeling of falling, sinking deeper into the bottom of my pit, as if it were quicksand. And just as I was about to go under, more than likely for good, I remembered God. If He truly is everything this young pastor says He is, maybe He would be willing to help. So I asked Him, "God, can you help me?" And in the midst of the turbulent, wave-crashing, jumbled-up thoughts in my mind, I heard a very calm "Yes." And in that moment, I knew I had to either trust God to pull me up or sink into the abyss forever. And without saying a word with my mouth, my mind said, *Okay, God, I need your help.* And immediately, I felt as if I had been pulled from the quicksand and was on solid ground. I was still in the pit, but at least, I wasn't drowning anymore.

A brief calm came over my mind as I started talking to God. Well, I say talking, but it was more like me telling God how messed up I am, how broken I am, how completely screwed up my life is, as if He didn't already know these things. But God let me ramble on, and in my ramblings, I became acutely aware of my brokenness, of a shattered life, and of just how desperate I was to be better.

As you might remember, just a few weeks ago, I was telling God of just how much I hated Him. Now I was going to these Bible studies with this young pastor, who told me I had to trust God, and even though I was learning a lot, the jury was still out for me concerning God. I was not really sure if He truly loved me, definitely didn't really trust Him yet, so it became more like me challenging God. "If you're really all these things the pastor says you are—loving, forgiving, all-powerful, nothing is impossible for you, and you do love me—then heal me. I want out of this pit. You say you can do anything, so let's do this! Get me out, heal me, and then let's get on with life. I've wasted enough of my life. Let's just get on with it and be done with it!"

So basically I said, "Bring it on, God!" Yeah, big mistake—the first year nearly killed me.

God was, like, "Okay, I'll bring it," and He bombarded me with emotions and feelings I knew nothing about. Everything I had been in denial about, every single feeling I had buried and didn't deal with, every emotion of everything I had been through, God laid them on me all at once! And it was devastating, overwhelming, shocking, unbearable, suffocating me to where I physically felt like I couldn't breathe, like an elephant was sitting on my chest. And yes, it took me a WHOLE year to admit defeat and give in and say, "Okay, God, let's do this your way."

Wow, be very careful what you ask God for and how you ask for it.

I'm super type A, very committed to my cause, whatever that may be. Once I make up my mind about something, that's it; I can't quit until it's done. You know, "get 'er done" mentality and completely ignorant and arrogant when it came to God. God put me in my place by giving me exactly what I had asked for, knowing full well if He hadn't, I would have questioned, doubted, and fought with Him on everything He was doing with me. God showed me exactly who He is—how He is all-knowing, all-encompassing, all-powerful, and not to be trifled with.

At the very next meeting, a new lady came with us, and after the worship and prayer time, she came over to me and said, "I need to pray for you." She motioned for my friend to come over and said, "We have to pray for her. There's something very dark and very ugly in her." As she started praying, she was moving her hands like she was pulling something out of me and praying that God would pull this dark, vine-like thing out of me by the root. When she finished, she just looked at me and said, "Wow, whatever that was, it was big and black, and it is gone now."

I left that church feeling like I could breathe again, like the elephant was gone. I got up the next morning with an ease that had not been there before, and as I went through my day, I realized depression had left me. God had done a miracle, and it was simply gone.

And so it began—a long, awful, horrible, painful, wonderful, amazing journey out of the deepest dark, a place where I truly was just a few feet from hell.

Grabbing the Rope

With the depression lifted, I was able to find enough strength to grab hold of the rope God had thrown down to me through this young pastor. I continued going to his meetings. He was now coming to the town I lived in. I would go to those meetings, naively thinking, *All right, this is it. God is going to heal me, and life will be good for the first time ever.* I was woefully unprepared for what would come next in my life.

Oblivious to just how much I had buried, to all the feelings and emotions of everything that I had gone through, and how well I had completely denied them, I completely ignored them—unwilling and unable to process any of them at the time they happened. But God knew each and every thought I had denied, every feeling I had buried, every emotion I didn't deal with, and one by one, he started the long arduous process of admitting them, dealing with them, processing them, and eventually healing from them. Absolutely, without a doubt, it was the hardest thing I have ever done. It was way harder dealing with and healing from all these hidden emotions and feelings than it was to actually live through them.

I would go to the meetings, hearing great and positive things, and leave the meetings feeling encouraged, emboldened, and even excited to face life head-on and get myself up and out of my pit, only to have life hit me so hard; I would lose my grip on the rope and smash hard back to the bottom of it. At first, I was determined to grab hold of the rope again, but day after day, week after week, month after month, bad things, tough things just kept slamming me. Just when I thought I was making some progress and a good break was coming, some catastrophe would happen, leaving me dazed and confused. It was horrible. Here I was, trying to run a business and make good decisions while trying to deal with dark oppressive thoughts, trying to face the emotions and feelings that I had buried so deep. It was never-ending and so very hard I'm not sure I can convey to you just how hard it is to go back and even admit to the atrocities that happened to me, let alone try to deal with them and heal from them.

And something that really bothers me is how people will casually and carelessly say things like, "Oh yeah, he or she was molested as a child, and they just need to get over it." For those of you who have never been molested or abused as a child, shut up. You have no idea what it's like to be raped as a child! Yes, that's right—raped! Oh, I know the polite thing to say is "molested," but the truth of the matter is that it's rape. And as horrific as it is for an adult to be raped, imagine if you will what it's like to be six years old and a grown man is on top of you, almost smothering you as he rapes you! You have no idea what's really happening, only that it hurts so bad.

Try to imagine the shame and reproach that sets in as you get older and start realizing how sick and wrong this is. How a family member or trusted friend completely destroys any sense of safety and trust. How being raped is a wound that goes straight to your soul and, if it's not dealt with immediately, turns into a large, gaping wound full of puss and infection that starts spreading to every fiber of your body, mind, and spirit, tainting every feeling, every thought, every decision. As the infection grows blacker and blacker, stronger and stronger, it chokes things like joy, peace, and your sense of security. And just like cancer, if untreated, it will eventually kill you. Maybe not physically—though for some it will—but for others, it may kill things like the ability to truly love someone, the ability to let someone in enough to be a true friend, the ability to trust or confide in someone, and, worst of all, the ability to ask for help. The shame and reproach are too much to deal with. The feeling of being vulnerable and unprotected is just too great a risk. If not treated, being molested as a child destroys the core of who you are—of who you are capable of becoming. It is by far one of the greatest weapons Satan has for destroying the essence of who you are—whom God created you to be. Women and men grow up with a sense of guilt and shame, and the older they get, the less likely they are to talk about it. And as long as you are hiding something, keeping it buried in the darkness of shame, it will never heal. The darkness will always have power over you and become a wide-open door for the enemy of your soul to come through at will and trample your thoughts and feelings, crushing right mindsets, right decisions, and right attitudes toward people, jobs—pretty much everything!

Of course, I was dealing, or at least trying to deal, with all these things and running a business. Outwardly, I was having success, but inwardly I was failing miserably. I struggled with admitting to all the things that had happened to me (in all honesty, I still do to this day). But God was persistent in drudging up old feelings and so much so that I started resenting Him. I would go to those meetings about Him and hear how loving He is, how powerful He is, how nothing is impossible for Him, how much He wants to help you, and how good He is. Then I would go home to one disaster after another, like the power company shutting off my power in the dead of winter because I couldn't pay my bill. Or having a young horse sold for a great deal of money, but in the morning when the people came to ride her, she couldn't stand up because she had foundered in her front feet, and no one could figure out why. Extreme founder causes bones in the feet to rotate, causing so much pain that horses are unable to stand or walk and must be put down.

It didn't take long for my resentment to turn to anger toward God. Here I was faithfully going to those meetings to learn about how good God is, only to go home and see absolutely no good thing from Him in my life. I didn't see Him helping me in any way, didn't see any good thing happening to me. But remember, the glass I was looking through was shattered, making everything look broken and skewed. From my perspective, God was cold, mean, and distant, putting an unbearable load on me when I just needed His help! I mean, I would go to the meeting and hear all the amazing things God was doing for the pastor—how he provided money just when he needed it, how sick people were being healed, how blind people could see again, and how crippled people got up and walked—only to go home and not have enough money to pay my bills and watch my brother die of cancer.

Once, those meetings had brought so much joy and encouragement to my heart—how he taught that if we would pray and believe in God, He would answer our prayers, how if we worshipped God and trusted Him, He would protect us and help us! And I did all these things the best I could, and still my brother died.

I began to dread those meetings, feeling betrayed by God every time I left them. I would angrily declare to never go back to another one! But three weeks would go by, and it was time for another meeting, and no matter how much I didn't want to go, something compelled me. Exhausted from working twelve-hour days, I would get up early and drag myself to the meeting, not even sure why I was going—a glutton for punishment, I guess.

The truth was, I desperately wanted to get better, to escape the pit once and for all, to be free from the dark thoughts of self-hatred and suicide. But enthusiasm dwindled as reality set in. I just couldn't see what good it was to drudge up all these old feelings and emotions.

I don't see the point, I told God. *Why won't you just please do one of your miracles and just heal me? Just take away all this blackness and hurt, just make it go away! Please, God!*

But He didn't, and I limped along, slowly losing strength and eventually the will to hang on to the rope and climb. It was just too hard. So I let go and slid right back to the bottom. My only prayer now was, "Please, God, just let me die."

Blinded by the darkness of despair, I could not see a way out. So deep was my grief that I had long ago lost sight of any light at the top of my pit. It was simply too far away, and all my years of clawing and fighting to get to the top had only left me exhausted and frustrated. I had tried in my own power and failed, and now I had tried God's way, and it was simply too hard, so I just let go. I was resigned to live and die in the darkness, very much alone in my misery. I succumbed to the fact that I had spent my entire life—up to that point—in a hole so deep and so dark that I was literally just a few feet from HELL, and now this would be where I died. Blackness engulfed me, and even with eyes wide open, I could see no light, no hope, no dreams, no desires. And so I closed my eyes and waited for death to come. I closed my eyes to all I had hoped to accomplish in life, closed my eyes to all the things I wanted to do, closed my eyes on ever being truly loved or of loving someone special. Yes, I closed my eyes, my heart, and my mind, and now to make death come quicker, I began to contemplate once again that suicide was my only way out. However, God had other plans for me, and this time, He Himself came right down to the bottom where I was lying and tied the rope around me, went back to the top, and began to pull.

I just hung at the end of that rope, though, too tired and unwilling to try and climb anymore. And eventually I just untied it and fell back to the bottom. But God was very persistent, and this time, He came down to where I was with a chain and a padlock, wrapped them around me, and, with great determination, started dragging me up the side of that pit, kicking and screaming because I couldn't get loose.

Oh boy, I fought with God, telling Him every day, "This is just too hard. I can't do this!" Undaunted, He just kept dragging me along. I whined and complained, had a huge pity party, but nothing worked. He just kept dragging me. I tried yelling and arguing with Him but to no avail.

It was awful. He just kept drudging up one horrible memory after another, not allowing me to move on until I had admitted it was real, and then worked through how I felt about it, processed it, and eventually got over it. It was so overwhelming, and I hated it! I tried in every way to close my eyes, look the other way, deny, and ignore like I had all of my life. But when God opens your eyes, it is impossible to close them! When He puts a thought in your mind, there is no way to ignore it! Yes, He totally pulled His God card on me, and I was powerless to do anything except what He wanted—what I needed. No matter how much I cried and whined, no matter how many times I told Him, "I just can't do this!" no matter how many times I begged Him to quit and just let me die, He was relentless, and I resented Him for it. I spent more time and energy arguing with Him than I did on getting better. I just wanted to quit. It's too hard, God!

I clawed at the lock around my waist. I squirmed and writhed and fought desperately to get loose, to escape the chain that was holding me, too miserable to even notice I was slowly getting further and further away from the bottom of the pit. The pit that had become my home, the pit where I resigned to live and die, the pit that was familiar. It was so familiar that it was easier to lie in the darkness of what was the same instead of risk failure reaching for what could be. Things continued like this week after week, month after month, year after year—me telling God how hard this was and God completely ignoring me.

No More Blaming

I was at yet another of those meetings when the pastor said something that would forever change my life, my perspective, and my way of thinking. He said, and I quote, "As long as you are blaming God, He will never change your situation."

Those words hit me like a board between the eyes! And as I pondered on what he had just said, a realization slowly started working its way into my thinking. As I thought about my situation, my attitude toward God, I realized that's exactly what I was doing. No wonder it didn't seem like anything was changing or getting any better. I can't really explain it, but it was like a switch was flipped in my head and new thoughts started rushing in. I had spent so much time blaming God, holding Him responsible for what had happened to me and so to responsible for my healing, that I missed something that now seemed so obvious. Healing and getting better was up to me. It's a choice. It's not up to God or anyone else; it's entirely up to me. I must choose every day, every moment, some days to be better. It's not God's responsibility but mine. God's responsibility comes in when I choose to believe Him that things can get better, that I can and will heal from what I've been through—when I trust Him. God is there to show me the way, show me how, but I must choose to let God in, choose to let God help. I must ask every day for God's mercy and love to be at work in me, to experience God's forgiveness that I might learn to forgive myself and eventually all that had wounded me so deeply.

This one thought of not blaming God completely changed my way of thinking, my perception of God, and ultimately my relationship with God. This one thought freed my mind in a way I never thought possible, opening my mind's eye to see things more clearly.

And as my mind started to think better, my eyes were able to see better, and it was at that moment, as I was hanging facedown at the end of that chain God had put around me, that I finally noticed something.

I was actually quite a ways from the bottom of the pit. Now I started squirming in that chain, not to break free but to turn around and look up. And when I did, I saw something astonishing, unexpected, and completely unbelievable! There in the distance was some light! Beautiful, glorious light! And light could mean only one thing—the top of the pit, the doorway to freedom, the escape from constant pain and suffering and the suffocating blackness. Barely able to believe what I was seeing, a small wave of hope coursed through my body, and I believe it was at that very moment the drag turned into a climb.

Hanging On

With great determination, I grabbed hold of the chain, put my feet against the side of that miserable pit, and started climbing. My feet slipped a lot, and my hands would grow weary, and more times than I care to admit, I found myself dangling at the end of that chain. But something had shifted in me. I had quit blaming God, finally realizing that it was not God trying to kill me but the enemy of my soul—Satan—who was out to get me. For if God had wanted me dead, I would already be dead. No, it was quite the opposite. It was Satan himself who had come after me as a small child and literally my whole life, trying in every way to destroy me, crush me, kill me, and it was God Himself who had been keeping me alive.

I apologized to God and asked Him to forgive me for wrongfully accusing Him all of these years. And if it wasn't for the pastor and that very wise woman I told you about earlier, I might still be blaming God. For in the midst of going to the meetings with the young pastor, I also went to one of the meetings that this woman had invited me to. It was at this meeting I learned about the true enemy of my soul, about how Satan hates God and so hates the people God created, how he wants to hurt God but, knowing he can't touch God, comes after the one thing God loves the most—us, His people. Knowing full well that God loves us with a love that is so all encompassing, so beyond what we humans can imagine or understand, he comes after us when we are young to crush us, destroy us, and kill us. And if he can't kill us, then at least he will hurt us so bad that it will affect everything else in our lives—destroying our dreams, our relationships with other people, and, for sure, our relationship with God.

Yes, between the teachings of those two people, I had a complete turnaround in my thinking. And so, when I found myself dangling at the end of that chain, instead of giving up, I knew I needed to ask God for help. And every time I did, somehow some way I was able to grab hold of the chain again, put my feet against the side of the pit, and start climbing. There were many times when it just got too hard. I was struggling and fighting to just hang on, let alone climb.

Many times when I cried out to God, "Where are you? This is too hard! I can't do it anymore!" God's reply was, "Of course, you can't. You can't do this on your own. You need to seek me every day, every moment if necessary. You are not strong enough to climb out of this in your own power. You need to trust me and ask me for help, and together we will get you up and out of this pit."

Ugh, there's that trust thing again and asking for help—two things I simply couldn't and didn't want to do. It took me a long time to learn that me holding on to the chain was my way of trusting God. Me keeping my feet on the side of the pit was me asking God for help. And as long as I did those two things, God was up above pulling on the chain. I hung on and, when God pulled on the chain, I moved my feet. Inch by inch, step by step, I was slowly making my way up the side of that pit.

And as long as I kept looking up—toward the light, toward God—He was faithful to keep helping, keep pulling on the chain. But unfortunately for me, there were times when I felt I would never escape the darkness and all too often found myself looking down at where I had been! And every time I looked back, I slipped a little, losing precious ground that I had fought so hard to gain. One thing I had been blind to was that the darkness had a chain of its own, and it was tightly fastened around me as well, constantly trying to pull me back, constantly pulling me down, and it was convinced that if it just pulled hard enough and long enough, it would successfully drag me right back to the bottom. And every time I looked back, I slid a little. Every time I remembered all the times I had already tried to get out and failed, I slid a little further. Every time I went back to old mindsets or ways of thinking, I lost a little ground. Every time my trust in God faltered and my faith seemed to disappear, I sank a little lower. But God, in all of His mercy, never faltered, never wavered in His belief in me, and would give the chain a hard jerk, yanking my attention back to Him. And as soon as I focused my gaze upwards again toward Him, I was able to start climbing once more.

Of course, now I had to climb hard just to get back to where I was, before actually making progress. This was how things went—me getting up a little faith to climb, losing my faith, and sliding down. Ugh! It was a painful process, but God never gave up on me, so I made up my mind that I would not give up either. Now I would leave those Saturday meetings with my faith all built up—ready to scale the side of that pit and get out only to have Monday come and life sucker-punch me in the gut, knocking the breath and faith right out of me and sending me careening down the side of the pit. As if God had lost his grip for a little while, only to grab hold after I had fallen a ways, stopping my fall as I hit the end of the chain hard.

I would just hang there for a while, trying to figure out what just happened, trying to just catch my breath. And with tear-filled eyes and a breathless voice, I whispered to God, "Why? What am I doing so wrong?" Knowing I couldn't blame God for what just happened, I reasoned that it had to be me. Maybe I was just inherently bad, and just as I had thought so long ago as a child, the same old feelings came over me. It's all me—nothing ever goes right because there is something wrong with me. And just like that, despair washed over me, and the darkness started to rejoice.

Eventually, God would give a tug on the chain, jolting me out of my own head, out of the past, and back to the present moment. He was reminding me to look up, so I would right myself in the chain, grab hold, and start climbing again. I fell many times during my climb. My past, the memories, and the darkness refused to let go, constantly tugging at me, constantly trying to drag me backwards. And all too often, I succumbed to them and would find myself hanging off the end of the chain once more. Having lost more ground, more time, more energy, I found myself in a life-and-death battle that seemed to never end.

Over time, though, I was discovering something about myself. Even as one battle after another kept coming at me, I was bloodied and bruised, but I was still standing. And I wasn't out of the pit yet, but I certainly wasn't at the bottom either. Looking back, I realized there was an enormous tug-of-war going on over me, and it truly was life and death. God was ever pulling me up to the light—to life, to goodness, to where dreams come true. And the enemy was constantly dragging me backwards toward the darkness—to death, to despair, to hopelessness. My part was to choose—would it be life or death? I chose life.

That sounds easy, choosing life, but it's not. For those of us beat up from the battle of life or scarred deeply by our past, it's a day-by-day, moment-by-moment choice. And for those like me who spent all of your life in the darkness, it's even harder because we are choosing something we know nothing about. We don't know what life free from dark and suicidal thoughts, from despair and complete hopelessness is like. From the prison of our own minds, we seek to be free, but after years of fighting, we are simply too tired to fight anymore. And even as horrific as the darkness is, at least it's familiar, which makes it very easy to just close your eyes and let go—let go of dreams, let go of desires, let go of life.

And unfortunately, that's where way too many of us find ourselves—battle-weary, bruised, bloodied, and completely worn out from the fight.

And it doesn't matter what you're fighting—some are fighting just to stay alive one more day, some are fighting to be free from their pasts, some are fighting alcoholism or addictions, some are fighting the hurt of divorce or the betrayal of a loved one. The list just goes on and on, but sooner or later, we all find ourselves in some sort of a fight all unique to us and our circumstances and yet exactly the same. What no one seems to want to tell us is that there is a tug-of-war going on over ALL OF US. And it doesn't matter if you're rich or poor, old or young, male or female, believe in God and Satan or not. There is a God who created all things, and He loves us with a love we humans simply cannot fathom. He sacrificed His only son for us so we could have a relationship with him, and Satan, an angel whom God created and put in charge of the music in heaven, was dumb enough to think he could throw God out of His own heaven and take over. So God threw him out and banished him to the earth. I don't know, but I think it takes a special kind of stupid to get kicked out of heaven. At any rate, he's here and he absolutely hates us simply because God loves us. Like I said, it doesn't matter if you don't believe in God; God still loves you and longs to have a relationship with you. You just become easy prey for Satan, and he easily manipulates your mind into all kinds of crazy and horrible things. He convinces a lot of people there is no God, and for the rest of us, he tries to convince us God doesn't love us and doesn't really care or that He's mad at us. All of it is a lie, like Jesus says in John chapter 8, verse 44, "For he is a liar and the father of lies."

Perfect Love

It took me a long time to believe that God actually loves me because for a long time, I didn't love myself. What I had gone through as a child rendered me useless and without worth. Through the actions or lack of actions by those who are supposed to love me, I grew up believing I was insignificant and didn't matter. My thoughts didn't matter, my feelings didn't matter, my dreams didn't matter—nothing about me mattered. And since everyone treated me the same, the only conclusion my young mind could come to was that there was simply something wrong with me. I was bad, and that's why bad things kept happening to me. This one thought infiltrated every fiber of my being, every thought I had, every decision I made; every single aspect of every single thing I did or thought in my life stemmed from this one thought. It wrapped itself around every good thought I ever had, every good idea, every good dream, every good decision I tried to make, growing tighter with each year that passed by and choking every good thought or plan or desire I had until eventually it killed all that was good inside of me. And what was vibrant and alive was now dark and dead. It filled me with blackness void of any dreams, joy, or hope, leaving me a cesspool of self-hatred, anger, and despair.

This was how I grew up. This was what shaped the adult I grew into. This was what my mind believed, and it didn't matter whether people liked me or not, whether I was successful or not; nothing mattered, and nothing—absolutely nothing—could make me like myself. No number of friends, no amount of winning, and eventually not even the love of horses could make me feel good about me.

That was the me lying at the bottom of that pit. That was the me that God wrapped the chain around. That was the me that God never gave up on, the me He had kept alive all those years. When

I tried to kill myself, God kept me alive. When others tried to kill me, God kept me alive. When I gave up and begged for death, God kept me alive. And why? Why would God keep alive someone who so desperately wanted to die? Well, I believe there are two answers to that question—one I will talk about later and the other one is love. God just loves us that much. We as humans cannot fathom love like that, and so we struggle to grasp hold of a God who loves like that.

For me and for any of you who have been wounded, we wrestle with the thought of love. Love here on earth becomes twisted and distorted. I mean, how can you say you love me and then walk out on me? How can you say you love me and then hit me? How can you say you love me and then rape me? You can put your own "How can you…" because we all have them. We hear all the time "I love you" while they're sleeping with someone else, "I love you" while they're talking bad about you behind your back—it just goes on and on. And if you're like me, you're thinking, *If this is love, then I don't want anything to do with it.* We become broken and hurt, and to protect ourselves, we put on anger and wrap a wall around us, keeping everyone at a distance, yet all the while deep down inside we long for love—real love, true love. Without love, we are empty and only a shell of who we could be, who we want to be. We keep looking to humans—broken humans just like us—to fill that deep desire for true love when we need to look to God, for only a perfect God can perfectly fill us with the love we so desperately crave.

Imagine for a moment if we all turned to God, if we all let God into our lives to heal and restore all that is broken, if we all allowed God to put a chain around us and pull us out of the pits we've been living in. What would the world look like then? What would love and forgiveness look like? What would all of our lives look like? Would anger and unforgiveness fade into the background? Would more dreams come true? Would hopelessness be lost forever? Would despair take a back seat to joy? Would we all learn to be better to ourselves and so better to others? And what if, just what if, we let God fill us with His perfect love? Would we learn to love others better? The answer to all of these questions is, "Yes, of course!" And this, I believe, is the other answer to the question I asked earlier. Why would God keep me alive? Why would God keep any of us alive?

For the most part, we—if we are honest with ourselves—are all the walking wounded. We all walk through life hiding our broken places, too scared to admit they're real, which would cause us to have to deal with them. No, it's much easier to just push them down and hide them under things like anger, working too much, pushing your body to be perfect, be thinner, be stronger. Or the opposite—eating too much, not eating enough, drinking too much, taking drugs to be happy, sleeping too much, blaming others. There's a million different ways to put a Band-Aid on the gushing wounds of our lives when the reality is we need to face them head-on so ultimately we can overcome them.

The thing we miss, though, is that we don't have to face them alone. There is a God, who created ALL THINGS—the universe and the stars, the earth, and all its creatures—who put the seasons in place, and who waits for you to turn your face His way. His name is Jesus Christ. He waits for you to just look His way and whisper His name. Just whisper, "Please help me." He waits every second of every day; as weeks go by, months go by, years go by, He waits. Having all the power and authority of heaven and earth—the power to *speak* the sun and earth into existence, the power to raise the dead to life, the power to completely and radically transform your life. All this power is at His fingertips, and yet He waits. For He has given us humans everything we have here on earth, and most importantly, He has given us free will. We get to choose every day what we will do, where we will go, what we will wear or eat. Every decision we make is because of the free will He has given us, so, too, we must choose Him—choose to know Him or not, choose to believe Him or not, choose to ask Him into our lives or not. And with ALL of His power, He is able to do anything—save all of us, change all of us, heal all of us—and yet He waits. He waits for an invitation from you to come into your life. And when you do, you've just tapped into all the power and strength of God Almighty Himself, the one who only had to speak a word and the earth was formed, the one who merely spoke and the sun and galaxies were created. He didn't have to lift a finger or break a sweat; He simply spoke all things into existence. We as humans have a hard time fathoming power like that, and yet ALL that power is just waiting for you to turn His way, for you to ask Him into your life, and then all that power goes to work on your behalf, to heal and restore every broken thing in your life. And because He loves you so much, He will never walk away from you, never give up on you, never ever leave you or forsake you! And just like me, you might try to walk away from Him, give up on Him, on yourself. He will simply come to wherever you're at. It doesn't matter how deep your pit is or if you are only a few feet from hell—He will come to you. And if necessary, He will put a chain around your waist and start hauling you up the side of your pit. Whatever that may be, whatever has happened to you, He can heal. Whatever mistakes you've made, he forgives. This is why you don't have to do ANYTHING alone, face anything by yourself, for you have a God who waits.

Unfortunately, many of us succumb to the darkness, to depression, to despair, and far too many die at the bottom of the pit alone in their misery and suffering. But for those of you who are still alive and reading this book, there is hope for you! No matter how dark your world is, how deep your pit is, simply reach up, for there is a chain just hanging there, waiting for you to grab hold of. There is a God waiting for you to look His way, and His way is always up. So if you find yourself in a deep dark pit, roll over onto your back, look up, and speak the name Jesus, and out of the darkness, you will be able to see the chain that is hanging there, waiting for you to grab hold of. And if you haven't the strength to hang on to the chain. Don't worry because God Himself will come right down to where you are, wrap the chain around you, and padlock it if necessary. And He absolutely will not quit till you are up and out of your pit. You need only to choose life. Moment by moment and day by day, keep choosing life, choose to look up to God. And when you find yourself looking down—down at where you've been—and you feel the darkness, the despair, the old mindsets, the old ways of thinking trying to drag you back to the bottom of your pit, just remember one thing: you need only to right yourself in your chain and look up. God will be waiting.

Gaining Ground

Every single day of my life, I thank God for not giving up on me—God knows I certainly did. I gave up all the time, gave up on myself, on God, on life. I had simply spent so much time in the dark, in despair, in hopelessness, I just physically and mentally did not have it in me to try anymore. But thankfully for me and for anyone else who finds themselves in a similar place, that's exactly where God steps in.

As I found myself lying at the bottom of a pit so deep and so dark that there was no light at all, the top was just too far away anymore for any light to reach me. As I lay there exhausted and broken, having tried and failed so many times, I refused to look up anymore. I closed my eyes and resigned to lie right there on the bottom in the darkness and die. And if my ears had not heard the sound of that preacher—the words that he spoke—I absolutely would have died in that hole, just a few feet from hell. When I didn't have the strength or the will to even open my eyes and look up, God sent a sound that penetrated the darkness and the distance that came all the way down to where I was. That wafted into my ears, into my consciousness, and gave me the strength to open my eyes and caused me to look up to see where the sound was coming from. And that was when I noticed the rope that God later changed to a chain hanging there. That was the moment my journey began—the journey out of absolute darkness and utter despair, out of self-hatred and anger, out of unrelenting pain and suffering. And it all began with a sound. So be careful what you are listening to, who you are listening to, for there will always be someone telling you, "You can't do that. You're not enough." Be careful of the voice in your head that has been lying to you all this time, the one that tells you, "You are a failure. You're not smart enough, strong enough, talented enough." The one that

JUST A FEW FEET FROM HELL

is always talking, always telling you what you can't do, desperately trying to drown out that one sound that says you can and you will, that one sound that causes you to open your eyes, causes you to look up to see where it's coming from, causes you to see the chain that's hanging there—your lifeline out of that pit, out of the darkness, out of despair, out of brokenness. You need only to take a hold of it and, with the energy you have left, speak the name Jesus.

Absolutely do not worry and take no thought about, "Do I have the strength to hang on? Do I have the will to hang on? Do I have the ability to hang on?"

Just reach for it, and God will do the rest. When God comes down to where you are, He is fully prepared—completely able and perfectly qualified to get you out of whatever is trying to kill you— for God has been with you all along. He created you. He knows you better than you know you. He knows all your dreams and desires because He gave them to you. The things you want, the passion you have for certain things, God put them there. You are perfectly and uniquely created to accomplish your heart's desires. No one can do it for you, and no one else can take them away from you. Oh yes, the enemy of your soul tries very hard to steal your dreams, kill your joy, and destroy your future. And for far too many of us, he succeeds.

He came after me as a child and did a damn good job at killing everything in me that wanted to live, sending one horrific thing after another to destroy me and kill my future. He filled my head with lies—lies that had just enough truth that I believed them. Yes, the hardest part of this journey for me was drowning out the voice in my head that kept telling me, "Things will never get better. You will never get out of this mess. No one cares about you. You should just kill yourself," constantly bombarding my mind with dark and oppressive thoughts.

But when I heard the words of that young pastor, words of life and love and of a compassionate God, it was like my ears, my mind, and my soul heard what I had been longing for—starving for—my entire life, and I didn't even know I needed it until I heard it. It was like God changed the channel in my head. I had been stuck on the same one for my whole life. It's like when you get into your car, and you have the radio on the same station all the time. You might change it once in a while, but mostly you have it on the same one all the time. If we're not careful, the same thing can happen to our minds. We get stuck on one station, and it's like our dial gets broken and we can't change it. So we just replay over and over the same negative stuff. All we hear all day long is what we can't do, that it's too hard, things will never change, we're not smart enough, we're too old to try now, we don't have enough money—on and on it goes. And when you hear, "You're not good enough," long enough, you start to believe it. So we have to change the station in our minds. We have to get around people and pastors who tell us we are good enough, smart enough, talented enough. We ARE enough because God made us enough!

Find a good church where they speak the Word of God or tune into Christian TV channels. There are some AMAZING pastors on Christian TV! I know because there is one I listen to ALL the time! When I first started going to the meetings with the young pastor, one of the girls who also went told me about a Christian TV channel, so I went home and turned it on, and there was a guy from Dallas, Texas, talking. I kid you not, but every single thing he said hit home with me! He became one of the three pastors that I listened to all the time. It was these three pastors—the young one from Africa, the one from Dallas, Texas, and the one at the church I go to—whom I allowed to speak into my life. I tried some others, but they really didn't fit for me, so these three became my new station in my head. They told me that I was enough. They taught me about God, whom I didn't really know and absolutely did not understand at the time and who, through their lives, showed me a better way to live.

The old station in my head did not go down without a fight, though. It kept constantly drowning out the new station I was trying to listen to. It was that one thought that was down deep inside of me, wrapped around the core of who I was, that still believed "I'm bad. Good things might happen to other people, but I'm bad, and only bad things happen to me." So when I heard the good word from the pastors, the truth about God and His promises to us, His love for us, I struggled to put them into play in my life.

And when I did get up a little courage to step out in faith, something devastating would happen and send me straight down the side of that pit. And once again, I would find myself hanging at the end of that chain, dazed and confused, wondering why. Why was it that when I tried to put into practice what I was being taught, it would all go wrong, and instead of gaining ground, I would end up sliding down? And immediately I would change the station in my head back to the old one and tell myself, "I'm never going to get out of here."

It took a long time and a LOT OF GOOD WORD to penetrate deep into the core of who I was, for the very essence of my being was under attack—being choked, strangled by that one thought: "I'm bad."

That one thought kept sending me down the side of that pit. Even though I was gaining ground, the light at the top was getting brighter and brighter. I knew I was getting close, but then I would find myself sliding and watching as the light got a little dimmer. I might hang at the end of that chain for weeks or until the next meeting.

Now remember, I chose to go to those meetings. Even though I didn't feel like it, didn't want to, I still made myself get up and go. And so must you. We have to choose to get better, and it's a choice we have to make every day.

Reaching the Top

Time went on, and I continued going to those meetings, listening to the pastor on TV, and going to my church. I got up early before work and read my Bible and spent time with God. And it was amazing— the more I made an effort to learn about God, the more He revealed Himself to me. The more I read His Word and His promises to me (to us), the more I believed. He promises healing and restoration to any and all who will ask and then believe. I read about all the miracles Jesus did while He was here on earth, heard about all the miracles the young pastor saw God do, and it caused me to believe. If God can and will do it for those people, then why not me?

At first, I had thought I needed others to pray for me. I mean, it was obvious that God listened to the young pastor, but I wasn't sure if He would listen to me. I still, deep down inside, thought there was something wrong with me. This one thought caused me to miss a lot of what God was doing for me, caused me to spend a lot more time in that pit. I would go to those meetings really hopeful and excited that the pastor would pray for me, and if he didn't, I would leave feeling sad, worried, and even a little bit angry. I was sad and worried because now, what will I do? Nothing good will happen now. And I was angry because I didn't get what I thought I needed, not realizing at that time God was doing exactly what I needed. It just wasn't what I wanted. I wanted the pastor, a good person, to pray for me because God listens to "good" people. But I was a bad person, and God would not listen to someone like me. I was my own worst enemy, and I didn't even know it.

But life would happen, things came up, situations arose, and I knew I needed prayer to get help to get through them. And since no one else was praying for me, it forced me to pray for myself. I was in a really bad spot one day when every single piece of equipment I needed to run my farm, my business, broke down. EVERYTHING ON THE SAME DAY! I mean, how is that possible? Every single thing I needed broke, and then my backup broke down too? ON THE SAME DAY! I didn't have enough money to fix all of them at once, and I had no idea what to do.

So I found myself outside sitting on a tractor that wouldn't run, crying, asking—more like begging—God for help. When my phone rang, I almost didn't answer it because I was so upset. Choking back the tears, I said, "Hello."

The person at the other end could tell something wasn't right, and she asked me what was going on. And I'm not sure why, but I told her, and she said, "Well, how about I wire some money to you and you just get everything fixed?"

I wasn't sure that I heard her right, and I was, like, "What?" She repeated herself, and I started crying again, thanking her repeatedly, and hung up. And then I started thanking God repeatedly, barely able to believe what had just happened. I was able to get all my equipment fixed and continued on doing business! That was a turning point for me. The situation forced me to have to pray for myself, and the real miracle to me wasn't that God fixed the problem by having that particular person call me right at that moment but that He heard me! God Almighty heard me. He listened to my cry for help, and He answered me! It was the most shocking, amazing thing ever! A holy righteous God would listen to the likes of me, a very broken and bad (in my mind) person? My faith grew three sizes that day, and the voice in my head telling me how bad I was had to shut up!

Now, to be clear here, God doesn't always answer prayers that quickly or on the same day. In this case, He did, but I'm pretty sure that God Himself may have been behind every single piece of equipment breaking down at the very same time on the very same day, forcing me to do something I didn't think I was capable of—praying for myself and God paying any attention. Yes, I believe God put the whole situation in motion, giving me the chance to learn to pray for myself, believe in myself, believe in Him, and then God got to show off to me on just how awesome He is!

I also believe that on that day, when my faith grew, God gave a mighty heave on my chain, and I flew up the side of that pit, stopping only a mere feet from the top. I knew I was close because the air had changed. No longer did I smell the stench of death and decay, but now fresh air filled my nostrils. And I drank it in, in huge gulps, filling my lungs with the freshness, the newness, the taste of freedom!

I continued going to the meetings, listening to the pastor on TV, and going to my church. I saturated myself with the good Word that these people taught. I made time each day to pursue God on my own, to sit and read His Word—the Bible—to pray, and to listen. Yes, listen. The more I sought to learn about God, the more He started speaking to me, for God's voice was the only thing that could drown out the voice in my head, which continually told me, "You're no good. God won't listen to someone like you. God would NEVER love someone like you." Yes, the truth of God's voice was slowly silencing the voice of my accuser. God revealed the truth about the lies I had been believing, revealing to me through the teachings of the pastors and the truth of God's Word, the Bible. God was showing me, telling me, what He actually thought about me. And what God thinks about me is exactly what He thinks about you. He loves us! He loves everything about us—the good, the bad, and the ugly! God is not shocked at the mess we get ourselves into. He is not surprised when we make bad decisions! And He is not angry at us for what we do because He knows that most of what we do is based on faulty information. Most, if not all, of our bad decisions are based on the lies we've come to believe—the lies the voice in our head has been telling us over and over for years! That's why He wants us to read His words that are found in the Bible! That's why He gives us good pastors who speak the truth about who God is and how much He loves us! That's why we need to ask Jesus into our lives so He can drown out the voice of lies in our heads and replace it with the voice of truth! And the truth is found right there in the Bible. There is promise after promise from God of how He will help us. He promises to heal us, restore us, and save us.

There is page after page of miracles Jesus did for ordinary people just like you and me. And the coolest thing for me isn't that He's able—I mean, come on, He's God and can do anything He wants! Absolutely nothing is impossible with God! No, the cool thing to me is that He's willing. An almighty and all-powerful God, who knows the name of every single star (think about that for a minute), is willing to take notice of me, of you. And not just take notice but also help me, heal me, save me. What an absolutely amazing gift we have—the one who holds the stars in His hands takes notice of us, just waiting for us to take notice of Him.

I pray that you won't miss it, the gift God has given us—Jesus Christ, Son of the living God. The One that can hold a star in His hand wants to hold you in His hand, wants to heal everything that is broken in your life, wants to restore all that has been taken from you, wants to drown out the voice of lies and fill it with His voice of truth. The voice that believes in you, believes you can get better, knows you can get out of your pit! And not only does He know you can, but He also knows *how* to get you out of whatever has hold of you—whatever is keeping you from living out your dreams, whatever has stripped you of your joy and peace, whatever has left you lying at the bottom of a miserable dark pit.

As the truth of God's Word started infiltrating me at every level, I was really able to climb. As the lies were being broken down one at a time, new truths were being put in place, and I began to heal. Slowly and steadfastly, God was replacing every hurt with His healing, every lie with His truth. He was slowly but surely going to work on the huge gaping wounds of my soul with surgical precision, knowing exactly what was damaged and exactly how to fix it, not only healing the obvious things that were wrong but also working on the very subtle things that I wasn't even aware of. He caused me to change my view on things, rethink some things—one of which was forgiveness.

This was one of the subtle things God worked on. Yes, probably it should maybe have been one of the obvious things, but for me, it wasn't. Although I hated the people who had hurt me so deeply, I really didn't spend much time thinking about them. I didn't think about them at all, actually. Like everything else in my life—don't speak it out loud, and then it didn't happen. Don't think about them or acknowledge them, and then it's like they never were. I was still living in a state of denial, and as a very wise man said, "You cannot overcome what you are not willing to confront."

Denial had become so easy for me I didn't even really have to think about it. When something bad happened, it was like my mind just dropped into autopilot and took control. Denial wasn't just a way of being for me; it had become a state of mind, subtly taking control of my thoughts, which ultimately governed my actions. And what had once kept me alive and kept my mind from splintering and destroying itself was now threatening to keep me stuck in this pit.

With God's help, I had learned how to confront the "things" that had happened to me. I learned how to acknowledge them as real and worked through how I thought about them, how they made me feel (by talking to God about them), and ultimately how to heal from them and move on to the next one. I knew I was healed when they lost their power over me. For example, there was a time when if I was watching a movie where a girl got raped, it would send me into a tailspin. I would get physically sick to my stomach and would have to rush to a bathroom and throw up. I could not finish the movie and wouldn't sleep for several nights and would spend days walking around, feeling out of sorts and anxious. It was horrible. Even if someone just mentioned the word *rape*, I would find myself not able to focus on work the rest of the day, not eating supper that night and tossing and turning in my bed all night.

These are the "things" God went to work on, revealing these deep hurts, and then, with unimaginable patience, love, and precision, went about healing them. Until a time came when the mention of rape did not send me into a state of panic and fear so real, I physically got sick. It's true I still don't like the word, and I must admit to this day it makes me uncomfortable. But I don't lose my focus, and I certainly do not lose any sleep over it. I can speak on the subject, and I can watch movies with scenes with this horrific thing in them while continuing to eat my popcorn, enjoy the movie as a whole, and then go home and sleep the whole night.

I don't exactly know how God heals such a horrendous wound to one's soul, one's mind, and one's character. What I do know is that the memories of this vile act once had me mentally and physically crippled and lying alone at the bottom of a deep dark pit, waiting for death. And yet thanks to God, now the mention of rape has lost its hold on me. And the darkness had to step back as God crushed the grip it had on me. God had taught me how to heal from the "things" that had happened to me, but now it was time to deal with the "people" who had done the things to me—people whose names I had not spoken out loud in years! Many, many years.

I knew God was talking to me about forgiving all these people because every sermon I heard was on forgiveness. If I went to one of my meetings, the pastor was talking about the importance of forgiveness. I would turn on the TV, and the pastor was talking about forgiveness. I went to my church, and guess what the sermon was about? Yup, forgiveness. And all of them were basically saying the same thing—the ONE thing that will keep you from receiving God's blessings, God's provision, and will keep you from accomplishing your dreams and desires is unforgiveness. As soon as I heard that, I knew I had to forgive each and every person who had done me wrong! Those losers were the reason I was in this miserable pit, but they certainly were NOT going to be the reason I stayed in this pit!

So with great conviction, I said out loud the name of each person and exactly what they had done to me and that I forgive them. The word *forgive* stuck in my throat, and I had to force it out several times, but I did it. When I got done, I did feel a little better not because all of a sudden I was super "holy" and now harbored no ill feelings toward these people. No, I felt better because God told me to do something and I did it. I think maybe it was the first time I actually felt a little bit good about me in a very long time.

Some time went by, and I thought I had a pretty good handle on things. I had (in my mind) successfully forgiven all the monsters in my life. I was healing well from all the atrocities committed against me, and I could now see the top of the pit. The darkness inside of me was being replaced by hope. Hope is an amazing thing. It's like a beacon of light that penetrates even the darkest dark. It spread through my body, pushing out the darkness, the oppressive thoughts, and the despair, filling me with excitement and expectancy and the sense that I actually could get out of this hole I'm in. And then right in the middle of this hope and excitement of almost being out of the pit, the flowers arrived.

Getting Out

It was a Friday afternoon. I had just finished working all the horses and was about to start my first lesson of the day when a girl that worked for me walked into the arena with a huge bouquet of beautiful orange flowers. Smiling, she said, "Looks like you've got an admirer!"

Surprised, I thought, *Who would be sending me flowers?*

The girl walked through the arena and over to the lounge area, where people can watch lessons from or wait for their turn, and set the flowers inside on a table. Curiosity got the better of me, and I asked the woman I was teaching if she would mind if I ran in and looked to see who they were from. She didn't, so I stepped into the lounge and noticed a large white envelope on the flowers and not the customary little card with the name of who they were from. I opened the envelope and pulled out a letter of several pages, thinking this was odd. I thought, *I don't have time to read all this right now*, so I flipped to the last page to see who had signed it.

And there it was—a name I had not seen or spoken in years, a name that immediately caused horrifying scenes to flash through my mind, a name that sent waves of nausea and fear through my body, a name I thought I was done with, a name I thought I had forgiven, a name I thought had lost its power with me. And then just like that, hope died. My faith seemed to leave me, and I found myself falling once again. The name was so shocking to my system, catching me so off guard, I was completely unprepared for the rush of feelings, emotions, and thoughts that smashed into my consciousness. I didn't even think to grab hold of the chain or claw at the sides of the pit as I went down. I was just in a free fall and might have gone all the way back to the bottom if God had not intervened. Once again, God stepped in and saved me, grabbing the chain and halting my rapid descent.

I gathered myself together as best I could and went back out into the arena to finish the woman's lesson. Of course, now she was curious and wanted to know who they were from, and in classic "Janel denial form," I causally replied, "Oh, they're just from an old acquaintance of mine who wants to catch up on things." I finished her lesson, giving no indication that anything was wrong. Working late into the evening, giving lesson after lesson, I finished my day with no one ever knowing I was hanging at the end of a chain, barely able to breathe.

That night in my house, I stared at that letter, those flowers, unable to open it and read it. I prayed, cried, prayed some more, and eventually found the courage to open the letter and read it. Having no idea what to expect, I was shocked to find out it was sent to me to say, "I'm sorry." Yes, the monster in my head, the boogeyman in the closet, the one who had raped me when I was fifteen years old, just said he was sorry.

Since this was the first time anyone had ever apologized to me, I had no idea what to do, what to think, or what to say. Then thinking I had read it wrong, I read it again and again, trying to figure out what to think about it, struggling with all the horrible memories and emotions of what seeing his name had brought upon me, and now trying to sort out what I thought about being apologized to. My mind was racing, fighting against all the negative, dark thoughts and feelings that were pouring into my head. They were thoughts and feelings that I thought I was healed from, was over with, and yet here they were, suffocating me, threatening to shut out the light, the hope, and, worst of all, to never let me get out of this damn pit yet again. How could this have happened? How could I have been caught so off guard?

Anger started to rise up in me. I thought I was healed. I thought I was over this crap! Here I was about to get out of this pit, and now I was right back in it. I fell far enough down that the stench of death was back. Darkness was all around me, and it was laughing. And oh my god, the old station in my head roared back to life, and all I heard was, "Who do you think you are? You aren't good enough to get out of here! You aren't strong enough. I told you, you would never get out!"

Oh, but God! He gave a hard yank on that chain, and I popped right up out of the darkness, out of the smell of death. Light and fresh air poured over me, and I remembered all the things God had been teaching me, all the things God had been working on. New thoughts rushed in. "You can and you will get out. You're so close now, don't give up!" Hope stirred and my faith came back, and as I was hanging from that chain, I stared down at the darkness and screamed, "You have no power over me because I forgave him!" Wow! I surprised myself!

All those dark, horrible thoughts and feelings were losing their grip on me. And while I did succumb to them momentarily, with God's help, I was able to rise above them and remember the truth of who God says I am and not stay in them. I truly was overcoming the darkness that had held me prisoner for so long. There was a time when that letter would have sent me straight to the very bottom of that pit, and I would have languished there for years. But this time, it was different. All the work and effort God put into me, all the meetings I went to, all the times I turned on the TV, and every Sunday that I went to church were now paying off. God had so filled me with the good Word of who He is and who I am to Him that there simply wasn't room for the darkness to stay.

Over the next few days, I was in a bit of a fog, reeling from all the emotions I had experienced just from seeing his name, wondering if the residue of what I went through would ever truly be off me. But I was encouraged that I had been able to rise up and get hold of those feelings and not let those feelings get hold of me. I was able to acknowledge them and then move through them to the other side— the other side where light and love prevail, where darkness loses its grip, and hope ignites a fire, that as long as you're believing and trusting, God will never go out.

I was at work again, just walking down the aisle of the barn, when the phone rang. I answered it, and the voice on the other end said, "Hi, Janel, this is—"

Unbelievable. It's the person who sent the flowers and wrote that letter. Shock washed over me, and I wasn't able to speak.

The voice continued, "I'm sorry to bother you at work, but I was wondering if you got the flowers and my letter. And how are you doing?"

The question "How are you doing?" snapped me back as indignation rose up in me. *You do not get to ask me how I am!* Anger took over in the place of fear, and I snarled back, "Why are you calling me?"

He answered, "Because I want to know if you read the letter." Then his voice started to shake as he continued, "And I want you to know how sorry I am."

I'm not sure what happened, but right in that moment, of his voice shaking and hearing him say "I'm sorry," something inside of me flipped, and it felt like one of the walls around me fell down. And I have no explanation for what happened next, but my voice softened, and I said, "Yes, I did. I got the flowers and the letter, and I appreciate your apology." My mind was racing, telling me to just hang up on him, you know, pretend it didn't happen. But my heart was telling me something very different, and it absolutely would not let me hang up.

He continued talking about how long he had been trying to find me, driven by the need to apologize. And then he asked me if he could meet me in person, wanting to say he was sorry face-to-face. Again, I have no explanation for my actions, but I said yes. "Yes, I will meet you in person." We agreed on a time and place and hung up the phone.

As soon as I hung up, reality smashed in, and I thought, *Oh my god, what have I done? Are you crazy? You can't meet him in person! You've spent your whole life trying to forget about him! WHY WOULD YOU DO THIS?*

As my mind started to unravel, one anxious thought after another, pouring in and fear gripping me, an unfamiliar calm washed over me. And very clearly, I could hear God's voice speaking to me, drowning out the old station, the fear, the anxious thoughts. And He said, "Janel, you told me that you've forgiven him. Now here's your chance to prove it."

Oh boy, I did say that, didn't I? It was much easier when I just had to go through and say names out loud and say I forgive them. But now I had to back up what I said. This might prove to be more than I can do. Immediately, I started trying to talk myself out of it, but deep down, I knew I had to do this. I knew God wanted me to do this, I knew He asked me to do this, and I knew in His Word He commanded me to do this. I also knew way deep down inside of me I needed to do this if I truly wanted to get out of this pit. And I did. My desperation to get out of the pit overrode my fear of seeing this guy, of being near this guy, and it compelled me to go to the meeting and once again look into the eyes of the one who raped me.

The calm that came over me as God started to speak to me remained on me. This was something entirely new for me. It was like God's love and presence were so tangible that I could touch them. He continued to encourage me and strengthen me, for as the day came when I climbed into my car to go to that meeting, I felt fear and reason trying to talk me out of it. My hands were shaking as I gripped the steering wheel, and I asked myself, *What am I doing?*

Deciding I wouldn't go, I looked for a place to turn around. That's when I noticed the song that was on the radio. Oh yes, it was about forgiveness. I found myself listening to the words of the song instead of turning the car around. When I realized what I was doing, I turned the radio to a different station, and guess what—another song about forgiveness. These are the words I heard: "The prisoner that it frees is you."

Okay, God, you're right. I need to go to this meeting. I don't want to, and everything inside of me is screaming to turn this car around. But I want to be free from this pit.

As I pulled into the parking lot of the restaurant we were meeting at, my whole body was trembling, and I absolutely did not want to go inside. I prayed and asked God for help, telling Him I couldn't do this by myself. Another wave of calm washed over me, and again I felt the presence of God surrounding me, encouraging me, and strengthening me.

I sat there for a moment, just drinking in the calm and gathering my courage. And then in my mind, I knew what I had to do; I told myself, "Suck it up, Janel. You can do this." And with that, I got out of the car and walked into that restaurant. The hostess greeted me and asked me if I was alone. I said, "No, I'm meeting someone," and she said, "I believe he is here."

As she led me to where he was sitting, I fought back the urge to turn around and run out of that place. Then she stopped and moved to the side, and there he was. A long time had passed since I had last seen him, and for a moment, I didn't recognize him, but then our eyes met, and instantly I knew those eyes. I smiled at the hostess and thanked her, grateful to have someone else to look at, but as she walked away and I sat down, there I was face-to-face with the one who had caused so much pain, so much suffering, so much shame, and so nearly cost me my life.

To say the least, it was a very awkward moment. Unsure of what to say, feel, or do, I had no point of reference for a meeting like this. He eventually broke the silence with some small talk. I struggled to respond, but thankfully our waitress showed up and asked us what we wanted to drink, and I was able to find my voice. I answered her, and as she left, I turned my attention to him.

Looking him straight in the eyes, I mustered all of my courage and began to speak. Determined to show no fear, no sign of weakness, no sign of anything, I answered his questions, and then I told him everything. As I told him what had been happening to me since I was six years old, tears welled up in his eyes. And as I continued with what he had done to me and how it affected me, how it nearly killed me, tears streamed down his face. I continued with what my dad had done, of how our former classmate had set me up with a violent rapist who tried to murder me. The words just came pouring out of my mouth. It was the first time I had told anyone everything that I had been through. The more I spoke, the more peace and inner strength I had, and peace like I had never experienced before welled up like a rising river, carrying me ever higher. New feelings started bubbling up in me—amazing feelings, the likes of which I had never felt before! They were feelings I couldn't really put a name to, but they were good! They were beyond good, they were miraculous! All this was going on inside me as I told my story. And at the end of my story, I looked this man in the eyes, and with heartfelt conviction, I told him I forgave him.

And no sooner than the words came out of my mouth the peace like a river inside of me swelled so rapidly I could feel it carrying me up and up with an amazing force! And just like Old Faithful at Yellowstone Park, it shot me right up and out of that miserable pit! It launched me so high I thought I might touch the sky! And when I came down for the first time in my entire life, I landed on solid ground! I stood there in the sunlight—the amazing, brilliant sunlight—enveloped by fresh air! And as I looked around, I did not see the cold, dark sides of a pit that nearly became my tomb. I saw trees and robins and beautiful green grass! I saw my hope restored, my faith renewed, and I saw something so new I almost didn't recognize it. I saw freedom! Freedom from a hole so deep, the flames of hell nearly swallowed me. Freedom from debilitating, dark, oppressive thoughts and emotions. Freedom from suicide, despair, fear, shame, anger. Freedom from everything that held me prisoner and kept me lying at the bottom of a pit. Undeniable, unbelievable freedom!

Amazing things were happening in my body as I sat across from the one who had inflicted me with an incurable wound—a wound full of poison and puss that had spread through my body, twisting and killing what was once alive and vital. Yes, as I sat across from this guy, things deep down inside that were twisted began to straighten. Where darkness had prevailed, light poured in, and what had been dead began to live again.

God visited me right there in that restaurant, right there in that booth, sitting across from one of the monsters of my past. Right there in the presence of my enemy, in the midst of darkness, God's mercy and healing broke free like a mighty rushing river, engulfing me in His love and forgiveness. It washed away years of despair and hopelessness, years of pain and anger, hate, and bitterness, and instead filled me with His peace—peace that passes all understanding, enabling me to see the monster in front of me as someone he loves too.

Yes, right there in that moment of what he had done and all that had happened to me as a result of it, the memories that had become like a stake through my heart and had pinned me to the bottom of that pit became the very things God used to lift me up and out of that pit.

I finished our meeting and left that place with a newfound sense of pride—pride that I had actually done it! I met with that guy and I forgave him! Not an arrogant pride. No, it was a feeling that maybe, just maybe, there was something good about me after all. Maybe the voice in my head truly had been lying to me all along. Maybe God really does love me, and just maybe I can learn to love myself.

As I was driving home from that meeting, something that had been dead and gone for years came bouncing back—joy, inexpressible joy—and I found myself giggling and laughing and I didn't even know why! My body felt light, and no one or nothing could wipe the smile off my face!

When I got home and got out of my car, I think I floated into my house. In fact, I don't think my feet touched the ground for weeks or months.

I went to bed smiling not only on the outside but also on the inside. When I awoke in the morning and opened my eyes, I was caught off guard when normally, as my mind was waking up and thinking about the day to come, there was ALWAYS a heavy feeling of dread upon me—so heavy it made it almost impossible to drag myself out of my bed. But not this day. The dread, the despair, the hopelessness were gone! Happy, positive thoughts replaced them for the first time in a long time—maybe ever. I was excited to get up and get going, excited to face the day, excited to just be alive! Yes, maybe the greatest miracle of all that God did for me was that I, Janel Hesson, was actually happy with being alive!

For as long as I could remember, I had longed for death. I had seen it as my only way out of the darkness, the only way to be free from that voice in my head, the only way to not feel oppressed by my own thoughts. My mind was crippled and tortured by horrifying images that NEVER ceased. All of my life I hadn't really been living; I had just gone through the motions walking around a black empty shell void of all joy, peace, or contentment. And unable to fix myself, I found myself lying very much alone in a pit so deep and so dark escape was impossible. Impossible for me but not for God. I am grateful beyond words that the Almighty God, creator of the heavens and earth, the one who spoke all things into existence, the one who holds the stars in the palms of His hands, looked down from where He resides and noticed me lying there in the darkness. He left His throne to come down to where I was and wrapped a chain around me. He NEVER gave up on me. He took the time to meticulously heal me from each and everything I went through. He healed my thoughts, my feelings, my emotions so completely that I find myself a completely new person—unrecognizable to myself.

Meeting that guy that day went from being one of the hardest things I ever did to being one of the greatest. It showed me I could face my fear and overcome it. I could face my monsters and defeat them. It taught me how to trust God in ways I never thought were possible for me and that it's "safe" to trust God, for He will absolutely NEVER let you down, NEVER forsake you, NEVER turn His back on you. And He will NEVER, EVER leave your side.

Free at Last

It took seven long years for God to get me up and out of that pit. They were the longest, hardest years of my life, for healing from all that I went through was much harder than actually living through them. Don't get me wrong, living through what I did was horrible and horrific and hard beyond what I could bear, and it's only in looking back that I see how God was with me all along. Back then, I did not feel His presence, I did not feel His love, but it was there just the same, surrounding me, protecting me. My mind, my body, and my emotions were so bruised and battered I didn't see God anywhere, but then I wasn't looking either. No, so dark was my mind, so lost was my soul, I never even thought about God. I never knew I could have a relationship with a holy God—a relationship that could heal me, change me, save me. Yes, living through what I did was hard, but even harder was learning to live with, overcome, and eventually move on from it. It caused me to examine all the thoughts I buried in denial, all the feelings and emotions I pretended didn't exist. It made me confront every single thing that had held me prisoner in a deep, dark pit, shoving me deep into the depths of depression and suicide, of despair so tangible you could touch it. It pushed me ever deeper into the abyss of darkness that causes you to make your bed just a few feet from hell.

So yes, those seven years were definitely hard and awful, painful and miserable, and yet so worth every single second of them! Healing and overcoming what has damaged you, what has crippled you, what has stolen your dreams, your desires, your hope, and what keeps you pinned to the bottom of a pit may be your greatest challenge, may be the hardest thing you will ever do, but it is so completely worth it. So worth getting out of the pit, so worth getting to the other side—to the other side of despair and hopelessness, to the other side of anger and bitterness, to where joy and peace live, where dreams not only come to life but also come true, where suicide and depression fall off you and hope burst forth.

For many of you reading this, words like *joy* and *peace*, *hope* and *happiness* may be as foreign to you as they once were to me. These are just things that happen to other people but not to someone like me, things that sound all good and well but aren't actually attainable for people like me. Well, my friends, that is the biggest and most dangerous lie you can believe. Love can fill your heart again, joy can return to you, and being happy can be a way of life for you. I know it for a fact. I know it as sure as you and I are breathing air. Because if God can heal someone like me, He can absolutely heal you. If God is willing to come all the way down to hell for me, then He will come to wherever you are too! God doesn't love me more. I'm not some super "holy" person on God's "good list." I am you—we are the same! There is just so many of us that are the walking wounded. Life shows no favors, and everyone goes through some kind of hurt, trauma, or loss. And for some like me, the hurt is so brutal it slashes a massive wound right through our soul, and we have no idea how to recover from it. We try in our own power. We try covering it up with a Band-Aid or simply deny it all together, but the truth is, there's a huge gaping wound in us bleeding out joy, hope, dreams, and desires. And if left unchecked for too long, you'll find yourself deep in a pit of despair, suicide, and despondency.

It's hard for me to put into words how glorious it was for me to get out of that pit, what it's like to see how blue the sky is, how green the grass is, to hear the birds sing again! To not dread every day of your life, to laugh and actually mean it! To find yourself humming and singing for no reason at all! To go to bed and want to wake up alive. To experience freedom from oppression, freedom from destructive thoughts and emotions. There are simply no words to describe the wonder of it, the awesomeness of it, the absolute miracle of it!

And with all of my heart, I would want you to also experience it. To experience God's healing is the most amazing thing possible on earth. It's so impossible for a mind that is entrenched in darkness to even fathom or imagine something like it. But once you've experienced

145

it firsthand, it's impossible for your mind to grasp all the infinite ways God has healed you. Every day you realize something new God has done for you, and just when you thought you couldn't be more grateful to God for what He has done, He shows you something else, and down to your knees you go and a new level of praise rises up in you.

For every dark moment, God shows me something bright and amazing. For every destructive mindset and decision, God shows me a new way to think and the ability to make good choices. For every hurt and misplaced feeling, God restores with love and forgiveness. There is simply no limit to the healing and restoration God can do in your life if you are but willing to choose Him, to believe Him, to trust Him.

Yes, for anyone who finds themselves in a dark place, maybe it's a pit so deep you think escape is impossible, or maybe you've been sucker-punched from somewhere out in left field and have been knocked to the ground. It doesn't matter; God has got your back. It doesn't matter if you've been struggling with it your whole life or for a few weeks. God is right there with you even if you don't feel it, waiting for you to just look His way. So if you aren't sure you'll make it one more day, one more night, or ever escape the darkness, please just turn His way, speak the name Jesus, and ask Him to save your life. Reach for the chain He throws at you and rest in the assurance that God is absolutely able to heal every dark place in your life, every trauma you've lived through, every horrific thing someone has done to you, every bad decision you've ever made.

Remember also that not only is He able, but He is also willing. Jesus did not come to this earth and die a horrific death so you could walk through this life beat down and miserable. No, He came so you could have an abundant life, an amazing life! He came and died so you could live! Because He came and died and lived again, so, too, shall you!

Me getting out of that pit is me living again! I was as broken and dead as anyone could be—dead to hope, dead to joy, dead to the possibility of being better. All my dreams were dead, and all the things I had hoped to do were dead. Everything about me was dead. My mind was dead to thinking good thoughts, good ideas, and my creativity was dead. My heart was dead, for a heart that doesn't love dies quickly. As I said before, I was just an empty shell lying there in the darkness, and as my soul—my spirit—was dying a slow death, God sent a sound that caused a spark. God sent a man all the way from Africa to tell me the truth about God. That truth became a chain, and that chain became my way out—out of the lies that had held my mind captive, out of the darkness that tried to kill me, out of the impossible into the possible. God is as real as the air you breathe. Isn't it true that you can't see air? And yet it keeps you alive. So, too, you can't see God, but it is Him who keeps you alive.

One of the greatest lies we as humans believe is that you have to be able to see it to prove it's real. So since I can't see God with my physical eyes, He must not be real. But then I would ask, "Can you see love?" and yet it is real to you—the love you have for a child, or a spouse, or for a pet. Can you put joy in a bottle and drink it? And yet it is very real to you when your child excels at something or you work hard at something and get acknowledged for it. Maybe it's a promotion at work, maybe it's simply getting a parking space up close when you've had a long day and you're tired. We are so quick to believe in feelings and emotions that we can't see and yet so quick to discount God as real.

Then there are those of you who believe in God, but you don't believe He's all that concerned with your life, your messes, and your dreams—which is just another lie straight from hell you've fallen victim to. You think He's too busy out saving the important people or saving the oppressed from dictators, you know, big things like that. "God doesn't care if I need help with my marriage. God doesn't care if I don't like my job—at least, I have one. God isn't concerned that I might not be able to pay my bills—I mean, God helps those who help themselves, right?" Oh my god, people! YOU'RE SO WRONG! Look at me! I was just lying there in my pit of despair, waiting to die. I wasn't doing anything, helping anyone! I wasn't praying some awesome prayer that got God's attention! I wasn't some "super holy," awesome person running around, doing all these great things so God would notice me! No, I was just someone whom life had eaten up and spit out, and I landed at the bottom of a very deep pit.

147

When no one else saw me dying in the darkness, when no one else noticed I was broken beyond repair, God did. God himself stepped out of eternity and into my pit! God brought all of His power and might, all of His love and light, all of His healing and forgiveness, all of His sovereignty and mercy right down to where I was. When I was too tired to open my eyes and see His light, He came, anyway. When I didn't have the strength to hang on to the chain He threw me, God hung on for me. When I didn't have the will to fight, God fought for me! When I didn't have the courage to face my fears, God became my courage. God became everything I needed. He stood for me when I lay there in a crumpled mess, and He stands for you. It doesn't matter if you're an atheist or Christian or if you've known God your whole life or never met Him before; God's love for you is as real as the air you breathe. God's love for you is so powerful it can raise you out of whatever pit you're in. Right now, you might not see a reason why you should go on living, but if you would but whisper, "Jesus, save me," God will show up, bringing with Him ALL power and ALL authority. The same power that raised Jesus from the dead just showed up in your mess, your pit. And He stands ready to breathe life into everything about you that is dead, to pour light into all of your dark places, to heal each and everything that is broken. My advice: let Him.

Sure, it's going to be hard, and yes, it will be scary at times, but because I have already gone through it, I can promise you it's so worth it.

I can also promise you God will not ever leave your side; you will face nothing alone.

If I can do this, so can you. It was never my goal to die at the bottom of a pit. I wanted to get out, wanted to be better, but I just couldn't get there on my own. Asking Jesus into my life, trusting and believing God to get me out of my pit was—IS—the GREATEST thing I have ever done or will ever do. And now it can become the greatest thing you will ever do. Oh, my friend, there's life after depression, after fighting suicidal thoughts, after despair, after hopelessness. And it is beautiful, wonderful, unexpected, and amazing!

Truly Out

I never intended to write this book, to have this story to tell—it was God who told me to write it. And at first, I told Him no, asking Him, "Why would I do that? Why would I go back and relive everything I just got over? It would be like jumping right back into the pit I just got out of! I barely made it out the first time. I am NOT GOING BACK there, God!"

Some time went by, and I was at one of those meetings with the young pastor, and he was praying for me when he stopped and said, "God just told me you have a story to tell." He continued praying and then, stopping again, said, "God told me again—you have a story to tell. Tell your story."

Of course, I knew exactly what he was talking about. Once again, God was telling me to write this book. And once again, I questioned Him. Why would I do that? What possible good could come out of reliving all of that horrible dark stuff? The truth was, I was terrified. I knew that to write effectively, I would have to go back and revisit everything I had gone through, revisit all those old feelings and emotions. I was absolutely terrified that if I went back into the darkness, this time it would win. This time, I wouldn't make it out.

Now that might sound stupid to you. After all, I've been talking about how it's safe to trust God. You don't face anything alone. God won't abandon you. And yes, all of that is true, and so true was my horror of going back into that pit! Yes, I trust God. Yes, I believe God can do anything. I know God did impossible things to save me! But so real was my fear of the darkness I had just escaped from. For the first time in my life, I didn't want to kill myself. For the first time in my life, I was free from hopelessness and despair. Yes, so terrifying was the thought of being back in that pit that my faith just seemed to shrivel up! Courage ran right out the front door, and I found myself lying in bed at night, unable to sleep because the darkness was whispering to me, "I told you, you would never be free." The old station kicked on in my head, and that familiar voice started speaking again, saying, "Where is your God now? What kind of loving God would ask you to go back?"

Full-blown panic was setting in when God showed up, rebuking the darkness and quieting that voice. He began speaking His truth to me, stopping my mind from completely unraveling. But I did have to ask Him, "Why would you have me go back there just to write a book? I don't understand, God." And again I asked, "What possible good can come from it?"

His reply was, "People are dying, Janel, people who need to hear your story. People just like you used to be languishing at the bottom of a pit. People that long to be free and see no way out."

So with fear and trembling, I picked up my pen to write, knowing that if God says good will come from it, good will absolutely come! If God says that telling my story will help someone else, then I believe it will.

I must admit I quit writing several times, allowing years to go by, when the pain was just too real, the memories too raw. I can remember working on the book on a Sunday afternoon and then Monday morning working horses and crying for no reason at all. I found myself fighting back the urge to kill myself, struggling to breathe as the darkness started to envelope me again. Terror set in as despair reared its ugly head, and I started crying out, "NO, GOD! No! PLEASE don't let this happen! Please, God, HELP ME!" God must have sent an angel to dispel the darkness, for the suffocating feeling lifted, and my heart that had been racing returned to normal, and my mind was able to think clearly again. As fast as the urge to kill myself came, it was gone, but the fear inside of me remained, and it would be years before I would pick up my pen to write again.

As time went by, I continued seeking God. I went to the meetings, tuned into the pastor on TV, and kept going to my church. I spent early mornings and Saturday afternoons reading God's Word and just spent as much time with God as possible, listening, praying, and writing down all that I heard from Him. The more time I spent with Him, the more my heart and mind began to heal. And I realized that it was time to pick up my pen for the final time and finish writing this book—finish telling my story.

I prayed long and hard before starting, and I never had another experience like I did that Monday morning in my arena. Never again did I feel the sudden urge to kill myself. Never again did my heart race as I struggled to breathe. Never again did the darkness envelope me. And never again did I face the terror of falling back into that pit.

For what I didn't realize at first was that as I was writing this book, God was rolling a huge, mountain-sized boulder over the opening of that pit. While I was sharing my story, reliving the hell I went through, God was sealing up the terror, the despair, the darkness forever. As I trusted Him, He was saving me again.

Once again, the very thing that terrified me—the one thing I was sure I couldn't do—became the very thing God used to heal me, restore me, save me completely. And just like the time I met that guy face-to-face and forgave him, launched me out of the pit! Writing this book sealed up that pit forever! Never again will I fear falling into it, never again will the blackness engulf me, and NEVER AGAIN will my past haunt me, hinder me, or terrify me. My past has lost its power over me and over my future!

So, too, this becomes my wish for you. For any of you who are in a pit, whether it's because of something someone did to you or because of a bad decision you made and you feel like you just have to live with it, it doesn't matter how or why you're in the pit, all that matters is that you realize there IS A WAY OUT! The enemy would have you believe you have to live with shame and regret, fear and anger, bitterness and unforgiveness. But that's a lie. The enemy will tell you there is no way out, that there is no hope, that God would never forgive you and would never help someone like you. All lies!

I am a living, breathing example of just how much God is willing to do for you—of how the lies of the voice in your head can cripple you, terrify you, keep you lying at the bottom of a pit, keep you from healing, keep you from living an amazing life full of joy and peace, full of God's grace and forgiveness!

Please realize this. Please, you really have to get this—GOD CAN AND WILL fix what is broken, restore what you've lost, and heal every hurt for EACH AND EVERY ONE OF US! It does not matter who you are, how old you are, how far gone you feel. NOTHING IS IMPOSSIBLE FOR GOD!

I've spent pretty much my whole life lying—lying at the bottom of a pit, lying in the darkness, lying in despair, lying in hopelessness, lying in anger. I was missing out on all the joy, love, and laughter life had to offer. I wouldn't wish that on anyone. You will never hear me say, "I'm grateful for what I went through," for that would be a lie. I hated every second of every minute of every hour I spent in that pit! I hated every moment of everything I lived through. But what you will hear me say is, "If God can use what I've been through to save someone else, then so be it."

It's true I am out of that pit—there's no more lying for me. No, now I stand. I stand in healing, in restoration, in forgiveness, in the ability to get out of the pit, to let go of anger, to forgive others. Yes, I stand healed, forgiven, and changed.

More importantly, I live! Now I live to see you stand, to see you healed, see you restored, and see you changed.

God's gift is free, my friends…
My story is real…
Use them and climb out of that pit.

About the Author

Janel Hesson started riding at age five on her pony. At age ten she trained and showed her first horse. At age sixteen she gave up her amateur status and turned professional. As an adult she started Janel's Training Center, which she owns and operates to this day.

She not only trains horses but also the people who love them. Working with children and adults. Teaching them how to ride, how to be safe around horses and most importantly, how to have an amazing relationship with—as she quotes—"one of the most amazing creatures God has ever created."

Janel also works with abused and troubled children, through riding and being around horses.

CPSIA information can be obtained
at www.ICGtesting.com
Printed in the USA
BVHW032032180721
612127BV00026B/890/J

9 781098 058517